Model Soldier Manual

D1744566

Edited and compiled by Chris Ellis

with contributions by
Roy Dilley and Bryan Fosten

Model & Allied Publications
Argus Books Limited
Station Road, Kings Langley, Herts.

ISBN 0 85242 448 5

First published — 1976

*Printed in England by
Jayprint (Holdings) Ltd, Thurmaston, Leicester,
for the publishers
Argus Books Ltd,
Kings Langley, Herts, England*

Introduction

ONE of the modelling hobbies which has caught popular imagination in a big way in recent years is the collecting, constructing, or converting of model soldiers and scale figures. Toy soldiers have always been popular as playthings for youngsters and there has long been a hard core of enthusiasts who were serious model soldier collectors. In the last decade, however, the fascination of model soldier collecting has been put within the reach of anyone interested in modelling, mainly due to the bigger output of kits and models, and their wider availability. Allied to the increased output of model products in this field there has been a good flow of books and reference works giving the vital information needed for uniform and equipment research. There are modelling articles in several hobby magazines, too, which deal regularly with aspects of collecting and modelling scale figures. The magazine *Military Modelling* is one of several journals in recent years which has appeared specifically to cater for the hobby. It is a fertile source of modelling ideas and information, and includes articles from time to time specially for beginners. It is not possible in a magazine, however, to concentrate solely on beginners' subjects, nor to keep repeating basic information. The object of this new book, therefore, is to present all the basic information on the hobby, its scope, and its potential. We show you the working scales, the materials, the tools, the painting techniques, how to start a collection of model soldiers, and much else besides. This book will be of special value to the beginner to the hobby or the complete novice, but it will have equal appeal to any established model soldier collector who wants all the basic information on the hobby in a handy size book at a price he can afford. All the information in this book comes from experienced modellers well-known to *Military Modelling* readers, and all techniques and materials described have been tried, tested, and proven.

Acknowledgements

We wish to thank the following individuals or organisations for help in the provision of information or illustrations for publication in this book: Airfix, Tamiya, Riko, Britain's, Historex Agents, Hinchliffe, Ensign, Humbrol, Greenwood & Ball, Old Guard, Rose Models, Series 77, Lynn Sangster, John Sandars, D.S.V. Fosten, R. Marrion, John Edgecumbe, H.R.W. Morison, Philip O. Stearns, B. Armstrong, Ray Anderson, Geoff Cornish, Roy Dilley, and Alec Gee, Editor of *Military Modelling* magazine.

Recent 54 mm scale metal 'collector' figures reach high standards of accuracy and characterisation; these officers of the 1890s depict Grenadier and Scots Guards in mess dress, from the Ensign range. Mess furniture is from the same range.

Contents

4

With many more master craftsmen now producing quality metal figures, there are fewer truly 'rare' pieces to be had. One of the pioneer figure makers whose work is still much sought after and who concentrates on some more unusual subjects in Holger Eriksonn of Karlstad, Sweden, seen here with his attractive 54mm figures of Napoleon and a French line infantryman of 1808 which have a distinctive style (courtesy H.R.W. Morison).

Left: Primitive peoples left plenty of evidence of interest in toy or model soldiers. This charming mounted warrior in clay is about 8 inches high, was found in Cyprus, and is dated at 700 BC.

1: The Model Soldier Hobby

THE representation of fighting men in miniature or model form is known to date back to earliest times; for instance, small scale soldiers and war chariots were found in the tombs of the Pharoahs. However, commercially produced figures for widespread public sale in what we would now call the 'toy' market date back only one hundred or so years, to the era of great industrial and business development in the latter half of the nineteenth century. German companies, selling 'tin' figures in flat, semi-flat, or 'solid' (full dimensional) form dominated the market at first with a prolific output. Toy soldiers became one of the most popular playthings for any Victorian boy and there was plenty of real military activity in the various continents of the world to stimulate boyhood interest. Then, as now, interest was international, and the casting of lead or tin figures was simple enough to place these early miniature soldiers among the first of the truly *mass* produced toys, exported all over the world.

In the early 1890s, the British toy-maker William Britain began producing a revolutionary new type of lead soldier which was hollow-cast. Apart from using less metal than a 'solid' cast figure, and so keeping prices low and competitive, the Britain's firm set new standards of quality, realism, and consistency of design. Britain's soldiers soon became the market leaders, though other firms using the hollow-cast process offered limited competition at times. Virtually any boy, anywhere, who liked toy soldiers in the first half of the twentieth century probably possessed or played with Britain's soldiers at some time or other. To this extent, Britain's, above all others, must have had an influential effect on the development of the modern hobby of making and collecting *model* (as opposed to *toy*) soldiers, for virtually all except the youngest of today's serious model soldier hobbyists must have had their interest sparked off by childhood gifts of Britain's toy soldiers, the range of subjects offered being truly tremendous.

In the 1930s the ranges of Britain's (and their competitors) were at their biggest ever. In this period the first serious attempts to set up clubs for model soldier collectors resulted in such organisations as the British Model Soldier Society and similar national organisations in other countries. As a sign of things to come, the 1930s also saw the first plastic-type figures appear (in Germany), and the first of the figures in ultra-miniature sizes (for example, Skybirds) came on to the market, starting the scales now most commonly used for wargaming.

In the 1950s, and even more so in the 1960s, plastic in its various forms became the principal material for virtually all mass-produced toy soldiers, rapidly displacing metal. By 1966 the last of Britain's once mighty series of metal figures had gone, sets of plastic soldiers in more restricted ranges coming in as replacements. Other firms, like Airfix and Starlux and Timpo also became well-known as producers of plastic figures for the toy market. In a few short years even these toy market plastic figures have changed in style

— the early top quality ones like those made by Britain's tended to be quite sophisticated and complicated, with many separate parts and elaborate pre-colouring; more recent offerings, though equally realistic, tend to be simpler to manufacture with fewer separate parts and are often simply one-piece mouldings.

Though the enormous variety of the old metal toy soldier days has gone for ever, today's youngster or the more serious hobbyist dependent on cheap model figures is still wonderfully served by the output of those firms producing for the toy market; their soldiers are to be seen in almost every toyshop or department store. And today's youngster or novice collector is the enthusiast of tomorrow.

The 1930s also saw the emergence of another type of miniature figure, the solid — usually cast metal — piece produced specifically for the serious collector. This type of figure was, and largely still is, something of a 'cottage industry' product. Production runs are short, prices are high compared to 'toy' figures, and availability is restricted. Some famous pioneer names in the field up to the late 1950s included Stadden, Gammage, Niblett, Greenwood & Ball, and Imrie-Risley. Because the production runs are low, most of these models acquired a scarcity value early on. These miniatures were true scale models, sold either as bare or primered castings for the collector to paint himself, or sold ready painted to a high degree of finish and accuracy at a commensurately high price. Only a few retail outlets, or the makers them-selves, offered these models and it is probably true to say that in the early days only the serious figure collectors really knew what was available at any given time. Except in one or two specialist shops, this type of figure was rarely seen by non-collectors.

Well into the 1960s there was no great change in the state of the model soldier hobby. There was a big output of 'toy' figures most widely purchased for children, though also collected or converted by serious enthusiasts, and a circle of makers producing connoisseur quality figures for a fairly small band of collectors who wanted something different from what the toy trade had to offer. Then in the latter half of the 1960s came a 'boom' of interest in military modelling which lifted model soldiers from a fairly obscure adult hobby into a pastime with a much more widespread following than had been known before outside the purely juvenile sphere. Model soldier collecting became 'respectable' and well-known, the old-established societies saw healthy in-creases in membership, and new societies were founded. Wargaming (which is really a specialist use of model soldiers) flourished as never before, and retail hobby shops began to stock model soldiers in kit and casting form in the same way as they had previously stocked model trains, model cars, model aircraft and other hobby material.

In fact military subjects as a whole shared in this 'boom', though here we are concerned only with scale figures. A big selection of new books appeared providing model figure enthusiasts with the essential information needed for accurate representation of uniforms and equipment, and model magazines started including articles on converting and collecting model figures just as they had previously dealt with model aircraft and other subjects. New hobby magazines were published — of which *Military Modelling* is a prime example — which catered specifically for the greatly enlarged interest in all things military. The output of new kits, accessories, castings, and paints was similarly increased until there was a veritable embarassment of riches for the model figure enthusiast, on a scale undreamed of by enthusiasts of only a decade or so ago. Not only the 'toy' side of the market greatly increased in output, offering very reasonable models at relatively modest prices, but there was a tremendous increase in activity by specialist suppliers with everything from high quality plastic figure kits (such as those made by Historex) to cast figures in abundance, and many accessories such as side-arms castings and preprinted paper flags and colours. Many new names became well-known in the specialist model soldier field, among them Hinchliffe, Lasset, Sanderson, Old Guard, and Cavalier. Model soldier collecting is now very much a popular hobby which is here to stay, well supplied with a constant stream of new products of every kind, supported by clubs, books, and journals, and offering a fantastic range of interest. There is a never ending output of figures and an almost limitless range of periods, uniforms, and modelling ideas which stimulate and maintain the interest. Collecting model soldiers, in short, is one of those hobbies which is never finished and the choice is vast, both in what you collect and how you go about it. You can spend no more than a 'pocket money' sum on every figure you collect, but if you so desire you can spend a small fortune; the hobby can be one of the cheapest you could possibly have, or one of the most expensive. The choice, again, is yours, largely dictated by the size of your personal budget and the spare time you have available. It is a hobby which can be — and indeed is — followed by a poor man or a millionaire with an equal degree of interest and output, if not expenditure.

In the pages which follow we show you some of the potential, the choice before you, and how to go about getting started. You may choose to follow any of the paths you wish through the hobby — time limitations alone will probably dictate a degree of specialisation — but it is not a bad thing to have more than one specialist interest, since if you get bored with one aspect of the hobby, a few weeks following another aspect altogether will allow you to return with renewed vigour to the first interest, and so on.

Toy or model?

One thing which must be clarified from the start is the distinction between 'toy' and 'model' as applied to miniature soldiers, for these two terms have been used extensively already in this introductory chapter. In the miniature soldier field, in fact, the distinction has for long been more of a descriptive marketing term more than an actual physical difference. Toy soldiers are produced, usually by big firms, in great numbers and at low prices for sale through toyshops largely to juveniles as playthings. Since the earliest days of Britain's first figures in the 1890s, however, nearly all the best quality 'toy' soldiers have been accurate enough 'scale models' by any definition, anatomically correct and usually extremely accurate in detail. This type of 'toy' soldier may well be painted in a simplified form, or even sold unpainted, but to any serious enthusiast with a limited budget the popular ranges of 'toy' soldiers may well constitute the basis of an entire collection. For each figure can form the raw material from which a unique collector's piece can be made for an almost nominal outlay. Those toy soldiers — and there are plenty of them — which are not obviously accurate in appearance can be simply by-passed by the keen collector, since there is no compunction to buy, but the proviso must be made that the collecting of 'toy soldiers' in their own right is a legitimate branch of the model figure hobby, and some hobbyists buy them, keep them, and display them as 'toys'. For example, old Britain's soldier sets in mint condition command huge prices in the collecting market and are regarded by many as an investment; indeed they are quite often sold in the showrooms like fine antiques.

What are variously described as 'collectors', 'connoisseurs', or 'scale' figures (and sometimes further dignified with the name 'figurines'), are those made for the specialist model soldier hobby market, the production runs of which are usually relatively low compared to the 'toy' trade, and the prices correspondingly higher. They may be sold painted, primered, unpainted, ready-animated, unanimated, assembled, part-assembled, or as a kit of parts depending on the maker. The best of these are very good indeed, impeccably detailed and anatomically accurate. Those sold painted are finished to a standard which justifies the high price. Conversely some of the figures in this section of the market are poor, actually inferior to so-called 'toy' figures, for it will be appreciated that the final appearance with either a 'toy trade' or 'model trade' figure depends to a large degree on the skill and touch of the craftsman who creates the master from which the production items are cast. If the master figure is poor, then the production items will be poor regardless of price and output. Most of these specialist production figures are in cast metal, but could equally well be in plastic or any other material. The famous Historex figures are typical examples of 'collectors' figures of high quality which are moulded in polystyrene yet are *not* mass-produced. In recent years, however, there has been a blurring of the distinction between 'toy' and 'model' even here, for firms like Airfix and Tamiya produce plastic kits of figures to the highest quality, appealing to collectors, yet selling at toy grade prices and turned out in thousands. So it becomes difficult these days to differentiate between a 'toy' and a 'model' and the keen collector is more likely to consider price, accuracy, and individual appeal of a particular model, rather than worry about its source of manufacture or point of sale. There is no real bone of contention here, for cheap but accurate kits and models have allowed the model soldier hobby to open its doors to all, and those who get a taste for the pastime by the wide availability of cheap but good items will then probably go on to seek out the more specialised limited run models as his collection grows. This, at least, appears to have been the trend to date. In the past there has certainly been a tendency among some collectors to look down somewhat disparagingly upon 'toy' soldiers, but there is room in the hobby today for models from all sources of origin. Certainly the judges in competitions, such as those organised by the British Model Soldier Society, do not make any distinction (unless, of course, a particular event demands it) as to the origin of any of the models in a contest.

The choice ahead

You are into the model soldier hobby as soon as you acquire your first figure. The biggest early decision is just what to collect from the vast selection on the market, made even more dazzling if you visit one of the larger specialist retailers who stocks all the popular ranges. There are hundreds of 'collector' quality figures available at any one time in a variety of scales, and even more 'toy' figures. Even if you had unlimited funds and all the time in the world you would not be able to collect everything available. If you are constructing and converting, a large element of time has to be taken up by research and practical work. So most newcomers are almost literally forced into specialising sooner or later. If undecided, however, spend a few months experimenting first to get familiar with painting, assembling, or converting techniques, depending on your involvement. Inexpensive kits and models like those by Airfix and Tamiya allow you to experiment a little while you get the 'feel' of the hobby without the need for a vast initial outlay. Early attempts are rarely wasted, for a poorly painted early figure can be repainted later on when your skills have developed, or unsatisfactory models can be 'cannibalised' to provide parts for later conversions.

Your direction may be conditioned by outside factors. Those who prefer wargaming may want to concentrate on small scale figures and be less concerned with detail and fine painting; the man who has already made tank models in a particular scale may want only a few good figures in that scale, primarily for use with dioramas involving the tanks; the apartment dweller may almost literally have only a shoe-box to accommodate all his models and may therefore choose a small scale but finish each model to a high degree of detail; you may want only a few very large scale but exquisite figures to display with a collection of weapons; or you may be lucky enough to have an attractive showcase, or space for one later, providing facilities for a true 'museum in miniature' showing off hundreds of figures. And, as mentioned before, limitations of finance may be an important factor restricting your purchases to the cheaper end of the market, though this is no great drawback with modern production.

Space and time limitations are usually dominant, and most hobbyists are happy to take some theme or period and collect, construct, or convert to suit. Popular areas include: Napoleonic Armies, British and Colonial 1880-1914, both World Wars, Wehrmacht period of 1933-1945, British regular and yeomanry cavalry, American Civil War, British Colonial Wars 1860-1900, and so on. Some modellers collect within more than one sphere of interest. The big collection of Roy Dilley, for many years President of the British Model Soldier Society, thus covers British forces since 1880, plus soldiers of all nations in both World Wars; hence there is 'overlap' as far as models of British troops are concerned in both the 1914-18 and 1939-45 period. Some collectors concentrate only on 'flats', others on 'toy' figures (notably Britain's) in original finish (restoring old models to the original condition). One noted modeller, John Sandars, has concentrated on the Western Desert campaign of 1940-42 with figures and vehicles of the time in realistic dioramas.

Perusal of magazines like *Military Modelling* will spark off scores of other ideas, for articles and illustrations covering every period crop up here and will feed your imagination. You will already, no doubt, have favourite periods of military history which will influence your choice. Some consideration of your own personal modelling skill and knowledge of the subject will need to be taken into account. For example, the hobbyist who concentrates on the Napoleonic era will find a rich collection of kits and models, and plenty of reference books all ready to hand; hence this is a good collecting theme for a beginner with limited resources and time. The modeller who wants a collection of nineteenth century figures, however, might have a tougher time. Most of the figures will need to be made or converted from others, and considerable research will be needed to find out the precise uniform details.

You may already have plenty of ideas for building up your collection — but if you haven't this book may further help you to decide.

2: Scales and Sizes

PART of the 'basic grammar' of model soldier work is to know precisely what scales and sizes are available, and which is the best for you. A good deal of confusion arises with some beginners who are already familiar with other types of scale model, because model soldier scales are most often quoted as sizes related to the height of the figure. Thus a model motor car may be described on the kit box as 1:32 (or 1/32) scale or a model tank may be described as 1:76(1/76), but a model soldier is not always described this way by the maker. Model figures will be most often advertised or described by size — 77 mm, 54 mm and so on. In fact, most of these mysterious-sounding sizes relate either directly or closely to common modelling scales, which is all to the good because it enables the imaginative figure modeller to look into other spheres of modelling activity as a source of supply for many accessories and constructional aids. This becomes specially important when you get involved in diorama(scenic) and conversion work. For example, if you were working in 54 mm scale and made a display piece showing a couple of soldiers resting in a barnyard, then it becomes an easy enough matter to visit your local hobby store and look for miniature plastic bales of straw — sold in model farmyard or slot-racing accessory sets as 1:32 scale items — provided you appreciate the relationship between the model soldier size and its actual scale equivalent.

It is usual to collect figures to a constant scale, following the convention with most modelling activities, if only because the uniformity of size of the models allows a visual harmony and gives a direct comparison of appearance from model to model. Obviously, there is nothing to stop you from collecting models in more than one scale, and if you come to figure modelling from other modelling activities (such as tanks or cars or railways) you may wish to go for figures which match your other interests in size and scale.

Many of the common current figure sizes derived, in any case, from the desire to furnish miniature figures which related to other popular types of model, and, indeed, the 'Grand-daddy' of them all, 54 mm, came about because Britain's in the 1890s produced sets of railway personnel as well as soldiers to match what was then the smallest size of model railway, Gauge 1, which scaled at 3/8 inches to 1 ft. The Japanese firm of Tamiya in recent years produced a range of plastic figures a little under 54 mm size specifically to match their range of 1:35 scale model tanks, and there are several other examples of an accepted model scale leading to model figures which match it.

Choice of scale is up to you, but it may be influenced by other factors such as:

Price — if you are working to a strict budget then scales in which the only figures or kits available are expensive may be ruled out unless you want only a very small select collection. The impecunious modeller may well opt for scales where there is an abundance of cheap plastic figures available.

Availability — in one or two scales the sources of supply are few and far between, and the output of models is limited, so the prolific modeller might find his activity restricted.

Skill — in some scales and ranges almost all output is in kit form and, of course, you need to paint your models unless you can afford to buy them ready painted; thus if your painting ability is restricted you may find small scale (or large scale) models frustrating depending on what you can or cannot achieve with a paint brush.

Space — as previously mentioned, lack of space may force you to concentrate on small scales.

Time — if you lack the sheer time for kit assembly or conversion, you may prefer a scale where there is a good selection of ready-made models.

As these factors are different for each individual we cannot advise further, save to say consider all these points, and visit as many stockists as you can to see what is currently on offer in the various scales. As many of the suppliers are small firms in the model soldier business, the hobby tends to be somewhat volatile. New ranges (and even new scales) are constantly introduced, others disappear from the market altogether, production runs tend to be short, figure designs are revised, and the fluctuating economic conditions of the hobby trade in general can change the supply situation from year to year and sometimes from month to month. This, incidentally, is why you need to keep up to date with what is currently available through the pages of a magazine like *Military Modelling* — both the reviews and the advertisements show the trend of the trade at any given time.

Here now is a summary of the most common scales: (we give the description first, followed by its scale equivalent)

54 mm/1:30 or 1:32 scale (3/8 inch, 9 mm, or 10 mm to 1 ft): The so-called 54 mm scale is far and away the most popular and common scale for model figure collectors. 'Toy' figures are produced in plastic by major firms like Airfix, Britain's, Timpo, Starlux and others; the old time toy soldiers by Britain's, Johilco, Crescent, and others were this size; and there is a prolific output of 'collector' quality figures, most in cast metal, by a great number of firms. 54 mm figures of some type or other can be purchased the world over. Names of ranges of 'collector' quality figures include: Lasset, Stadden, Rose(Gammage), Hinton Hunt, Sanderson, Greenwood & Ball, Old Guard, Cavalier, Imrie-Risley, Cameo, Superior, and many others, all supplying metal models, and Historex, Airfix, Tamiya, Helmet, and Segom (plus others) in plastic kit form.

54 mm offers a convenient size for storage and display, the models can incorporate a great deal of fine detail, and they are big enough to make painting a task within the capability of an average modeller of some experience. Most model and conversion work is done in this scale, and probably 80-90% of all collectors prefer 54 mm size. There are several firms also who specialise in making, animating, and painting 54 mm figures to special order and they can be found in magazine advertisements. Within the 54 mm size there is truly something for everybody — a host of cheat 'toy' figures suitable for adapting and converting, assembly kits, and plenty of ready-made pieces. In addition there are dozens of accessories in the model car, aircraft, train, and farm

The same figure drawn to actual size for the main model soldier scales, showing comparative sizes. If in doubt, place a figure on this diagram to determine its scale, making allowance for some height variation (drawing by Stephen Heap).

20mm   25mm   30mm   54mm   75/77mm   90mm

animal spheres which can be adapted and used for conversion and scenic work.

What will be noticed, however, is that there is a fair amount of actual size discrepancy between models which are all nominally to 54 mm size. While the pioneers of this scale worked to 3/8 inch to 1 ft more recent introductions have tended to choose rather larger scales (9-10 mm to 1 ft) which makes for a rather taller, bulkier figure, up to as much as 60 mm high (the size describes overall height less base and headgear). In addition, Tamiya and some other Japanese firms produced smaller figures (matching 1:35 scale) which are rather under 54 mm in height. As real people come in differing heights and bulks, however, these variations in size are no great problem except where there is a blatant visual descrepancy which offends the eye. In diorama work, judicious placing of slightly smaller figures towards the rear can actually be an advantage in emphasising perspective.

Summing up, the complete beginner will probably find 54 mm scale the best overall choice which takes most factors into account.

20 mm/1:86–1:90 scale (3.5 mm to 1 ft): This is the favourite miniature size of figure most used by wargamers who require model soldiers en masse

Above: A typical metal kit figure in 54 mm scale, shown assembled. This is an English Civil War 'roundhead' cavalryman by Phoenix. Below: Three of the fine metal 30 mm scale figures by Suren (Willie Figures).

for table-top battles. An extensive range of cheap sets of these figures was pioneered by Airfix, but there are other plastic figures to be had. Numerous firms produce in metal (these figures are rather more expensive) including Hinchliffe and Rose, and there are many accessories which match the scale. It corresponds to HO gauge model railways, so that the hundreds of building and scenic kits made for model trains in this scale can be utilised, as can miniature motor cars, trucks, trees, farm carts, and so on. There is a big selection of accessories directly intended for military use too, including ruined buildings, fortifications, artillery, and horsed carts. For the modernist, the entire ranges of Roco-Minitanks and Roskopf tanks, plus other lesser known firms are all to this common scale, so the potential is enormous. While wargamers use these pieces extensively, there are many modellers who simply collect the figures and paint, convert, and detail them most exquisitely. A tiny 'mini' diorama could be built within the tray of a matchbox, and a complete horsed gun team is only a few inches long. Obviously in this small scale there must be some limitations of detail — muskets, for instance, are commonly over-scale in thickness, face features are often merely suggested, and so on, but the overall effect can be very pleasing. Prices are low, even for the cast metal figures and the plastic Airfix-type figures are the cheapest of all.

25 mm/1:76 or 1:72 scale (4 mm to 1 ft): This size is really a development of 20 mm scale with the figures grown a little larger. The modern origin of the size appears to have been in Britain. Airfix introduced a series of military vehicle kits to 1:76 scale in 1960; this scale, at 4 mm to 1 ft, matched British 00 gauge model railways (which are slightly larger in scale than international HO gauge railways). 20 mm scale figures looked slightly under-size alongside the Airfix tanks, and later Airfix figures (and some made by other makers) were increased in size to compensate. Cast figures are also now common to 25 mm scale, covering all periods, and Skybirds figures introduced in the 1930s were the pioneers in this size. Much the same as 20 mm figures in all other respects, 25 mm soldiers have the same potential and are used mainly for wargames and small dioramas.

30 mm/1:60 scale (5 mm to 1 ft): While figures of this size were once the most favoured wargaming type (now largely supplanted by the 20/25 mm size), they are, perhaps, less widely collected now. Those figures which can be had are mainly of the 'collector' quality cast metal type, Suren(Willie), Stadden, Minot, and Phoenix all being superb ranges. These fine figures are all exquisitely detailed, and being much less expensive than 54 mm cast pieces, they are will worth consideration by anyone seeking an economic but select collection of high quality. The size lends itself well to compact but striking diorama work. A few cheap plastic soldiers to this size are sometimes to be found. Many 'flats' are to this size.

35 mm/1:52 scale (6 mm to 1 ft): This again is really a variation on the original basic 30 mm size and the same remarks apply. Available ranges are fairly limited.

40/42 mm/1:42 to 1:48 scale (¼ inch or 7 mm to 1 ft): A fair number of figures are produced to this scale which matches 0 gauge model railways and the limited numbers of 1:48 scale military vehicles and model cars which are on the market. Much of the output is in plastic by the makers of the tank kits

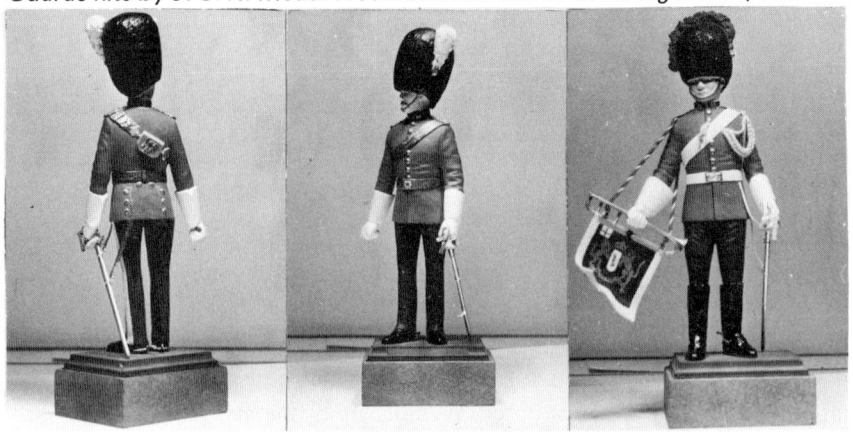

Models in 1:12 scale ($\frac{1}{2}$ inch to 1 foot). Above, left: Knight of Augsburg from Aurora kit; note real feather plume and armour shading. Above, right: WAAF of 1942, a complex conversion based on Airfix parts. Below: Scots Greys officer (two views) and trumpeter converted from Airfix Guards kits by J. S. R. Mead. Note real material used for aigulettes, etc.

Right: Very large 1:6 scale figures like 'Action Man' or 'Fighting Soldier' (shown here) are intended as toys but can make accurately detailed display pieces. US soldier in M1943 equipment is complete with eating utensils in haversack. Above: Typical accessories made for 1:6 scale soldiers — all accurate and including uniform items from actual cloth material. Below: 40 mm figures sold ready assembled and painted for collectors — French light infantry colour party by MDM in hard plastic.

INFANTERIE LÉGÈRE - Bataillon de Neuchâtel 1807.1814 Voltigeurs

19

made in this scale. Some metal figures can also be had, and there are some 'civilian' figures intended for model railways which offer military conversion potential. Some 'flats' are to this size.

75/77 mm and 80 mm 1:24 scale (13 mm or ½ inch to 1 ft): A fairly recent size in the model soldier world, these are similar to 54 mm, mostly being cast metal 'collector' figures of very high quality (eg, Series 77, Stadden, Hinchcliffe, Tamiya). The larger size allows for excellent 'super detail' work and these can be most attractive pieces. Prices are higher than for 54 mm figures, of course. A few plastic figures can be found, mostly in 1:24 or 1:25 scale tank kits.

90 mm/1:20 scale (15 mm to 1 ft): Relatively few figures of very high quality can be had in this size. Stadden is the main range, but there are others. Price is, of course, fairly high.

15 mm/1:120 scale (2.5 mm to 1 ft): A quite recent innovation, these figures are virtually miniaturised versions of the 20 mm type figure, but the pioneer range in this scale (Laing) offered excellent quality and realism. Though a wargamer's size, the figures lend themselves to ultra-miniature diorama work. Prices are low due to the small amount of metal in such tiny figures, but painting and converting demands a fair amount of skill. Scale is equivalent to TT model railways.

5 mm/1:350 or 1:300 scale (about 1 mm to 1 ft): Another recent introduction to meet the demands of the wargamer working in the ultra-miniature scales of 1:300, 1:285, and 1:350. These figures mostly come in groups (eg, a marching company, or a gun and its crew) due to the minute size. These tiny scales allow vast numbers of troops to be employed in wargames. Prices are low, but the figures are representative rather than finely detailed due to the small scale. The non-wargamer might find them useful for a 'gimmick' type diorama — say Trooping the Colour on a tea-tray — but these are very much for wargamers.

9 mm/1:160 scale (1.9 mm to 1 ft): Figures of 'civilian' type are available in some variety as accessories for the popular N gauge model railways. At the time of writing there are Scruby(USA) military figures in this scale, but it seems inevitable that more must come sooner or later, following past precedent where model figure sizes evolve from established model railway scales. There is a big range of N gauge scenic accessories, buildings, vehicles, etc, already available, which can be used for wargames scenery and diorama.

1:12 scale: Generally referred to by this name, these figures are mostly available in plastic kit form from firms like Airfix and Aurora, and are not necessarily of military subjects — Kings, Queens and personalities are commonly depicted. However, the kits can provide raw material for conversion to other figures, and good work has been done by a few collectors specialising in this scale. Occasionally large plastic figures ready-made in this scale are to be had, and there are some specialist producers who will make models this size to order.

1:6 scale: Figures this size are usually of the jointed 'mannikin' type, of which the 'Action Man' series is the best and most common example. Though intended for the toy market, the uniforms and equipment supplied are generally highly accurate and there is a select band of enthusiasts who

Though 20 mm scale figures are mainly used for wargames, they lend themselves equally well to collecting, being economic in both cost and space. These metal British 24th Foot of 1815, neatly painted and detailed, occupy a space of only 4 inches by $1\frac{1}{2}$ inch.

collect these models and, indeed, feature them in large dioramas. In addition to the 'Action Man' range there are others of this type, some to a smaller scale (about 1:9) but similar in style. The clothing is made of real material, simulating the original very realistically, and there is good conversion potential.

Other scales: One or two makers produce in scales which are largely unique to their own products. Thus Elastolin make excellent hard plastic ready-painted figures in about 64 mm size (pioneering the large size in a sawdust-and-glue composition substance before World War 2). Various figures are to be had from time to time in plastic, metal, or porcelain which do not fit into any of the commonly collected sizes. The model press usually records any new items of this type which appear. Some 'flats' are produced in odd sizes and there are occasional off-beat items to be had, such as card cutouts.

3: Types of Figure

AS we have seen, scale military figures come in a great variety of scales and sizes, and the preceding chapters have indicated the different styles of figure which have appeared over the years. There are actually many different approaches to building up a collection, and while magazine articles and books on the subject often give most emphasis to the constructional side of the hobby, it is quite possible to be a model soldier collector without ever having to get involved in practical work. Let us look at the different types of figure available and see what the scope is in the various categories.

Flats

Starting chronologically, we first have models in what some would consider their most primitive form — the flat two dimensional 'tin' solider which is the earliest of the commercial types, dating back to the 19th century, as a commercial product but going back to antiquity as a type of miniature figure. Examples exist from Roman, Egyptian, and Mediaeval days, but the classic type of tin figure (zinnfigur) or tin soldier (zinnsoldat) collected today has its origins in Nuremburg where pewterers and tinsmiths used scrap material to make toy soldiers for their children. In the early part of the 18th century some commercial production was under way — a few moulds survive from about 1750 — and this had become quite well established by the late 18th-early 19th century, Nuremburg and Furth being the great centres of production. Early sizes were haphazard, 70 mm or 55 mm being known, but by 1848 the maker Heinrichsen brought out 30 mm figures which became the most popular, and probably the first ever recognised scale for miniature figures. Among collectors of Flats, this is known as the Nuremburg Scale; by contrast producers in Berlin and Hanover standardised on 40 mm size and this size is sometimes called Berlin or Hanover Scale.

The classic flat zinnfigur was — and still is — engraved in slate moulds, the two slates involved having the 'back' and 'front' engraved directly into the surface; suitable channels for the 'tin' to run in are also engraved, these runners being broken off when the figure emerges from the mould. The two slate moulds are pegged tightly together for the casting process. The whole process is relatively simple, very much lending itself to 'cottage industry' but the secret of success is in the artistry of the original engraver. Most makers sold their figures in sets, nicely presented in flat boxes and painted in the factory. Production of Flats is still very much a German industry, even today, and output is still surprisingly prolific. In the English-speaking countries Flats have never enjoyed immense popularity but there is a faithful following outside their countries of origin and interest seems to be growing. There are today, for instance, a few retailers in Great Britain importing Flats. Flats today can be had either painted or unpainted, and the 30 mm and 40 mm sizes still predominate.

One aspect of Flats is that their very nature allows whole groups to be moulded as a single piece — for instance a single base might feature a war elephant with its riders, plus outriders on horses, or a horsed gun team will

Above: Two typical boxed sets of 30 mm Flats shows the huge variety of this type of figure, in this case 'ancients'. Below: Completely scratch-built 54 mm figures by Arthur Woolford, made from Isopon over wire armatures—a Wren, ATS girl, and WRAF.

come as a single piece. Over the years Flats have very much reflected social history. While interest might be largely centred on model soldiers, just about every aspect of life — civilians, circuses, fire brigades, farms, and even complete buildings have been produced in Flat form and this sort of non-military item may still be had. Though two-dimensional, the beauty of the Flat is that it looks three-dimensional from the normal viewpoint due to the skilful engraving. Careful painting, with highlighting and shading judiciously applied, can enhance the appearance even more. Dioramas do not need to take up much depth, for trees and background items also come as Flats. A diorama can be made in little more than the depth of a picture frame, and some astonishingly good work of this kind has been exhibited. Prices compare favourably with those for 'collector' quality cast models and Flat collecting certainly has a charm and appeal of its own, reflecting the rather gentler artistic approach to model figures of well over a century ago. Some very old moulds are still being used to produce ranges of Flats, so one can actually purchase a little of model soldier history at the present time. Some modern subjects are obtainable in Flats — time has not stood completely still — and one very attractive recent range by the firm of Rucker of Hanover covers the various Werhmacht forces of the World War 2 period, all in 40 mm size. Scholtz, Aloys Ochel, and Neckel are among foremost makers of Flats today.

Half-round Figures

Half-round (halbplastich) figures also mainly originated in Germany in the 19th century, and were a logical development of Flats, made by engraving more deeply into the slate moulds. Many of the makers of Flats also made halbplastich pieces and some of the major producers was the prolific firm of Heyde. Though this firm made models in many sizes, the 40 mm size was the most popular line and these figures are sought after by collectors today. The half-round figure still has a following from those who collect vintage models. The firm of Kober of Vienna produces half-round figures to 40 mm size from moulds first made in the 1890s and the big range available represents many types and regiments from the days of the Austro-Hungarian Empire, including the Kaiser and his staff, and civilian 'society'. At least one Scandinavian firm produces a 'home moulding' set for producing half-round figures, with a number of different types of mould.

Anyone interested in either Flats or Half-round figures will find it well worthwhile to invest in a large book *The Collector's Guide to Model Tin Figures,* by Edwin Ortmann (Studio Vista, London 1974) where the subject is dealt with in exhaustive detail. Here we can only give you a taste of this fascinating subject.

Card cut-outs

Allied somewhat to Flats, and also reminiscent of a bygone era, is the card cut-out figure. Some full dimensional card figures have been produced, but the most usual type of cut-out figure is simply a flat representation with a tuck-under or separate base. In the old days, and occasionally even today,

Above: These are 40 mm scale half-round figures of the 1890s now produced from original moulds by the firm of Kober, Austria. The sets shown here are Bosnian-Herzogovenian infantry and their band, together with a field officer. Note the traditional Austrian pony cart for the bass drum. *Below:* Now rare collector's items, these are card cut-out Grenadier Guards of the 1890s, about 77 mm size and full colour printed. They originated in Germany, in this case for the British market.

colour printed cut-out figure sets have been produced commercially. In the 19th century, card (or even paper) cut-out armies were popular. In recent years a very nice range of cut-outs to 30 mm size was designed and produced by the late Rene North and these can still be obtained. These are line illustrations which have to be painted by the purchaser. It is worth mentioning that anyone can make his own cut-outs of this sort by tracing figures from suitably sized, illustrations of soldiers. This type of model may seem crude in this age of cast 'collector' figures, but cut-outs are not be to sneered at. Realistic dioramas (of the Flat type) have been made in card, and skilled painting is required. The great virtue is cheapness — you can use water colours from a child's paintbox, and the North cut-out cards for instance, are quite inexpensive.

Vintage toy figures

The old type of lead toy soldier that is now long out of production has become an ever more popular subject for collection. These figures were produced and played with by the million until the last of them disappeared from their maker's lists in the 1960s. In Britain the big name, and the biggest range, was, of course, Britain's whose output started in 1893. Britain's are famous for their 54 mm 'standard' size, but they also made 20 mm ('Lilliput'), 40 mm ('W' series), and various big 75 mm and 90 mm pieces in their time. Several past catalogues have been reproduced in facsimile form and give the modern collector a good idea of what was available and when; in addition several books deal with Britain's figures in some degree of detail. The range not only included hundreds of model soldier sets, but also covered guns and equipment, a circus, zoo, farm, Boy Scouts, footballers, a fox hunt, and many other miniatures of contemporary British life. With the disappearance of these very realistic and charming toys from the market a fair size collecting fraternity quickly grew up, seeking out pieces second-hand and scouring attics and junkshops. Most figures now command premium prices, though bargains and 'swops' can be had, and some mint pieces now cost more than new 'collector' quality cast figures. Quite regular showroom sales are held and anyone with a big collection of Britain's figures has a good investment. Some notable large collections have been built up, one being that of John Ruddle, Hon Sec of the British Model Soldier Society, who has an example of nearly every Britain's item ever produced. Some collectors restore battered old models to their original condition, by repairing and repainting. Any enthusiast wishing to start a collection of Britain's models in today's conditions can, in fact, do so most cheaply by buying broken models and restoring them. B.S. Armstrong, in *Military Modelling Annual 2* (MAP/Argus Books Ltd, 1975), provided a very useful article dealing with the restoration of Britain's models. Armstrong like John Ruddle, also has an interesting pastime of making the broken figures into the regiments which Britain's did not themselves ever produce. This is done by changing the details and colours as required. John Ruddle has produced elephant batteries and cycle troops which look as though they were produced as Britain's sets but are, in fact, made up from old broken models converted and painted in the Britain's style.

Above: Mint condition Britain's metal figures are a popular collecting item. Shown here are Royal Company of Archers (captain), line infantry, 1815 British infantry (sergeant), and Fort Henry Guard (officer). Below: Restored Britain's metal figure finished as a trooper of Canterbury Yeomanry — not in the original Britain's range (B. S. Armstrong).

27

Johilco, Timpo, Charbens, Crescent, and others all made metal toy soldiers like Britain's though never so prolifically, and these, again, are sought after. Heyde (Germany), Mignot (France), and various other countries made figures very extensively, and these are also attractive to the toy soldier collector. Lucotte and Mignot in France pioneered 'solid' (ronde-bosse) figures on a big commercial scale early in the last century.

In addition to their intrinsic value and interest as toy pieces, the commercial metal toy soldiers were used as the basis for conversion work by the older generation of model soldier enthusiasts when there were very few alternative sources of material. Roy Dilley and Henry Harris were two pioneers of the techniques and performed marvels of re-animation and alteration which changed standard Britain's castings out of all recognition, and their collections were largely built up in the 1940s and 1950s from converted Britain's items. Many of their conversions have been illustrated in books and magazines over the years, and some are included here. Anyone with a supply of old Britain's models can emulate their method — and many do so — but enthusiasts coming new to the hobby in the last decade or so will find this prospect rather academic due to the lack of figures now.

While the Continental toy figures were cast solid, the main British producers used the 'hollow-cast' method. The metal was poured into a cool mould, then as the outer metal hardened in contact with the mould, the still-molten metal on the inside was 'blown' out, so giving a hollow shell, and the tell-tale 'blow hole' in some part of the figure is a well-known characteristic. There was, of course, great economy of metal and the figures were relatively light and fragile, so that broken heads, stands, and missing arms were the normal hazards of childhood. Modern restorers are often faced with the need to replace the broken pieces.

There were a few other toy soldiers, mainly of curio value now, such as printed tinplate figures in two halves which were clipped together with tabs in the normal tinplate way, and plaster, wood, or composition pieces. Mention must be made of the fine Lineol and Elastolin figures of the 1930s which were mostly in a composition substance over a wire core. These ranges concentrated (though not exclusively) on the armed forces and political organisations of the Third Reich, the figures being about 65 mm in size. They are, again, now highly prized collector's items.

Modern toy figures

The modern equivalents of the old cheap lead soldier are the relatively inexpensive plastic figures now sold in most toyshops, but also to be had from some model shops. Britain's continue their tradition with plastic, as do Timpo. Another major maker is Airfix, producing in both 54 mm and 20/25 mm sizes, but there are many others which will become apparent to the diligent searcher, including many 'bazaar' type items from anonymous Far East factories. The most common toy figures are excellent and largely accurate scale models in their own right, while some are dismally inaccurate. Some toy figures come ready painted or pre-coloured, others being sold unpainted. The plastic used in these figures is usually of the soft, flexible type, the reason for this being an economic one connected with speed and ease of moulding. It gives a strong, almost unbreakable piece but brings a few minor disadvantages which have to be overcome by any modeller using these as source material for conversion work. From the modeller's point of view, these modern toy figures open the door to serious model soldier work at no more than pocket money prices, and some well-known modellers rely almost entirely upon them. John Sandars, for instance, is internationally known among model soldier fans for his fine work but virtually all his figures are converted from Airfix and Britain's 54 mm 'toy' figures or similar pieces. The availability of such good basic materials really does make the model soldier hobby one of the cheapest of all constructional hobbies. The most common flexible plastic used for toy soldiers is Polythene, but more recent Britain's figures (and some other makes) are in PVC (Poly Vinyl Chloride) which is vastly superior.

A worthwhile point to make is that plastic toy figures are already beginning to become collector's pieces, just as the old metal toy figures are today. Britain's, for instance, quite frequently change their product lines and some of the earlier plastic releases, like the 'Eyes Right' range, are even now collector's pieces with their second-hand value now well above the original retail price. Shrewd collectors will have already put aside boxed sets of obsolete Britain's plastic sets, for posterity!

Collector's figures

Cast metal figures made in short production runs for discerning collectors, appear to date back to the 1930s and originated in Great Britain. Richard Courtenay (with some very famous medieval pieces) and W.Y. Carman were two pioneers but there were others. Their effort coincided with the formation of the British Model Soldier Society, when serious enthusiasts began to organise themselves. Some very famous names which have appeared since are Charles Stadden, Norman Newton, Greenwood & Ball, Eriksonn, Niblett, Russell Gammage (Rose Models), who between them set the early standards for this type of figure. The great model soldier boom of the past decade has seen many more 'names' appearing in Great Britain, USA, Spain, and France, among others. Soldat, Lasset, Series 77, Cavalier, Superior, Imrie-Risley, and Old Guard are among very well-known names, but it is almost indivious to list these only for there are so many others. Some producers go out of business, others start up, new ranges are offered by established makers, etc. Most of the accepted sizes of figure can now be had as cast metal 'collector' figures. Perusal of current hobby magazines will keep you informed of what is on offer at a particular moment.

These 'collector' figures are cast in a white metal alloy which can actually vary from maker to maker in its actual constitution. Lead is a part constituent of the alloy, but in recent years the tin content has been much increased by most makers, partly to obviate 'lead disease' — the oxidisation of the lead which ruins the figure — and partly to overcome objections on health grounds. Many modern figures are in technical terms pewter or near pewter. Most of these figures are first made as unanimated masters, that is the basic figure is modelled by the sculptor with legs apart and arms slightly splayed. Allowance is made for shrinkage in the mould and the really skilled designer

Among early metal 54 mm 'collector' figures were these Greenwood & Ball German Army types, distinctive and attractive even though now overshadowed by more recent and better detailed models.

Above: Though somewhat crude by modern standards, the Greenwood & Ball Lancer and Life Guards officers are true 'collector' pieces for the connoisseur of metal figures. Below: Typical modern metal 'collector' figures sold ready-animated; Luftwaffe pilot, Kriegsmarine seaman, and German Marine, all by Lasset, 54 mm scale.

is the man who can actually compensate for mould limitations in the master so that the moulded figure then appears anatomically correct. The mould is usually a two-part vulcanised rubber item; figures may be made either by 'sludge casting' whereby each piece is made individually by hand (pouring the molten metal into a runner hole in the mould), or by centrifugal casting on a machine where a certain degree of (relative) mass-production is possible. The unanimated figure fresh from the mould is then animated by altering leg and arm positions, adding side-arms or any other equipment (by soldering or glueing), and positioning the figure on a base which is either cut from sheet metal or made as a separate casting. As each moulding is individually animated, no two figures need be exactly alike — the same basic soldier might be turned out with rifle at the 'order', the 'trail', or the 'high port', for instance, with only a minimal change in limb positioning. Some figures are sold in kit form with the unanimated moulding, accessories, and base, together with assembly instructions; most are sold ready-animated and with a flat primer coat of paint. However, many makers offer a service of painted and specially animated figures to special order if, of course, you can afford the price.

The alternative to the above system is to produce the model from the mould as a straightforward metal assembly kit, already animated where limbs and head and other parts may be separate mouldings. A degree of variation in animation is possible even here, for a running limb may be cut through and re-cemented to give a different angle. Figures of 54 mm scale and above are usually sold in this kit form style as an alternative to a ready-animated type figure. In the smaller scales the figure will probably be sold cast complete with base moulded in ready-animated positions, but the maker of the smaller wargame size figure often offers many alternative action positions.

Because rubber moulds are used, they wear out fairly quickly, and the designer may then alter his master before making new models, or make a new master altogether. Models which do not sell well enough may never get a second production run, and so on. Output per individual model could be anything from 100, 250, to several thousand depending on its popularity, and the diversity possible is enormous. Because there are so many models to choose from now, the days of real rarity are virtually gone. If one maker stops producing a particular regimental figure then the chances are someone else does a similar one. However, there are some delightful models produced and the collector who can afford the outlay and who has the time and skill for all the painting involved can build up a superb collection of quality figures, eschewing all reliance on toy figures. The price is, of course, at the other end of the spectrum from the toy figure. For the cost of a typical single dismounted 54 mm cast metal 'collector' figure, one might purchase at least ten, and as many as 75 toy figures depending on the maker and type.

The advent of plastic construction kits, which are cheap but accurate scale models, added another element to the model soldier world. Plastic kits of aircraft, cars, and ships became really numerous in the 1950s, and in the 1960s the firm of Historex in France extended the idea to the 54 mm soldier. They have since built up the most exquisite range of Napoleonic era soldiers of great diversity and taking advantage of the nature of plastic moulding they

Representative of the high standards now being achieved by the makers of commercial cast metal 'collector' figures is this set of German Imperial Heavy Cavalry types by Series 77. Left to right: trumpeter of Saxon Guard Carabiniers, Garde du Corps standard bearer, adjutant of line cuirassiers, Garde du Corps officer, trooper of guard Cuirassiers, sergeant major of line cuirassiers, officer of line cuirassiers. These are 77mm high pieces, 1:24 scale.

can offer models of hitherto unbelievable detail, right down to separate badges and buttons. Because Historex is a fairly small company offering a big range, and with a 'spare parts' service for scratch-builders too, Historex kits cost nearly as much as a cast metal 'collectors' figure. In recent years, however, Airfix have come into the market with hard plastic (polystyrene) figure kits (quite distinct from their polythene 'toy' soldiers) which are similar in style to the Historex kits, yet at little more than pockey money prices. The range is restricted, but growing, and these Airfix kits undoubtedly offer the cheapest entry to the 'collectors' quality type of figure yet known, at least as far as 54 mm scale goes. Many who start with the Airfix kits can graduate to Historex kits, or cast metal kits, as their experience grows. Segom, Helmet, and Tamiya are other firms offering plastic kits of similar type and at varying prices, and it is worth looking out for others. Some 'civilian' type figures in constructional form are included in various plastic car and truck kits, and offer conversion possibilities as soldiers.

Eriksonn produces figures in 30mm, 40mm, and 54mm sizes. This 54mm Swedish line infantry officer of 1860 is typical of his work, the sculpting of the horse being particularly noteworthy.

Special figures

Outside the main classifications are a few miscellaneous types. There are one or two craftsman working in modelling clay, like John Cuiffo, who makes 54 mm models to order using Plasticine. The actual colours are derived from the basic Plasticine colours and the models are not painted. Others make in Plasticine, 'curing' it with Banana Oil and then painting it in the normal way. In theory anyone would make his own home-made figure from Plasticine, but it is a great art which is beyond all but the most skilled of sculptors. Some other skilled makers offer their services (at a commensurate price) in making figures to special order.

A few years ago, when figures were much less readily available than they are today, it was quite popular to attempt to make one's own master (say by converting an old broken toy figure) and then moulding figures at home with a rubber mould. If you are the practical type, there is nothing to stop you doing it still, provided you have domestic approval to use the gas ring, and like doing this type of work. The technique has been described and illustrated in many books and magazine articles and will not be covered here; a good illustrated exposition of the work involved was given by Philip O. Stearns in his book *How to Make Model Soldiers* (Hamlyn, 1974).

Finally, it is interesting to note that some metal figures are now to be had in die-cast form, of which the Britain's firm offers attractive Guardsman and Beefeaters, and some are made by other firms. Unlike the old lead-based figures, these are in hard Zamak (a zinc alloy) so they are not really convertible due to the brittleness and hardness of the metal. They are of passing interest to collectors, however.

4: Tools of the Trade

EVEN if you start in model soldier collecting merely as a purchaser of ready-made and ready-painted figures you may well want to alter paint-work and details, or arrange models in realistic groups. In short, whether you originally intended to or not, you are likely to get involved in constructional work sooner or later. For the average modeller this usually starts off by the purchase and construction of a plastic or metal figure assembly kit, and the beginner is certainly advised to start like this, as a kit normally has detailed assembly instructions and all you need for the model is normally included in the packet. A common alternative is to obtain a plastic 'toy' figure and con-vert, detail, and paint it, or you may buy a ready-made 'collector' figure and wish to alter it in some way to give it a personal individual touch.

Whatever path you take is going to require the use of tools suitable for working with model figures. Fortunately, like so much else in this hobby, the sort of tools you need are not too expensive and once some basic ones have been procured, anything more elaborate can be acquired later as funds become available. For assembly of a typical plastic or metal figure kit, you can get along nicely with the following:

(1) Modeller's craft knife, and at least one spare blade.

(2) A fine file — this can take the form of an old nail file, emery boards, or one of the special 'rat-tail' or 'mouse-tail' files.

(3) Tweezers.

Of the above, craft knives are widely available; prices are modest but get the best you can afford. Multicraft, X-acto, and Swann & Morton are among the brand names to look for. Start off with a medium handle and a selection of straight and round edged blades, and always try to keep at least one blade in reserve unused for the very important jobs where the cleanest possible cut is needed. Old blades can be kept after they are past their prime, for they are always useful for scraping work. Check blades from time to time and replenish your stock when needed. As time goes on, both a light handle and a heavy duty handle would be desirable additions to your tool stock, since there can be occasions when either a hefty or delicate knife is useful in speeding up particular tasks. Some more advanced modellers favour surgical scalpels for light work, and these can be obtained from medical supply shops.

Files of the 'needle', 'rat-tail', or 'mouse-tail' type are most useful for cleaning up joins and apertures in an assembled model, and for lots of other tasks in conversion work. Try to get at least one and work towards a selection of two or three of varying size. As a temporary measure, and certainly quite adequate for plastic kits, emery boards are very useful substitutes; they usually come with coarse or fine faces, are exceedingly cheap, and can be cut or broken into slivers of a size suitable for any task. Even when you have a file to hand, there is always a use for emery boards.

In the case of tweezers, these are fairly essential for model soldier work where delicate parts like epaulettes might need to be positioned and held in

35

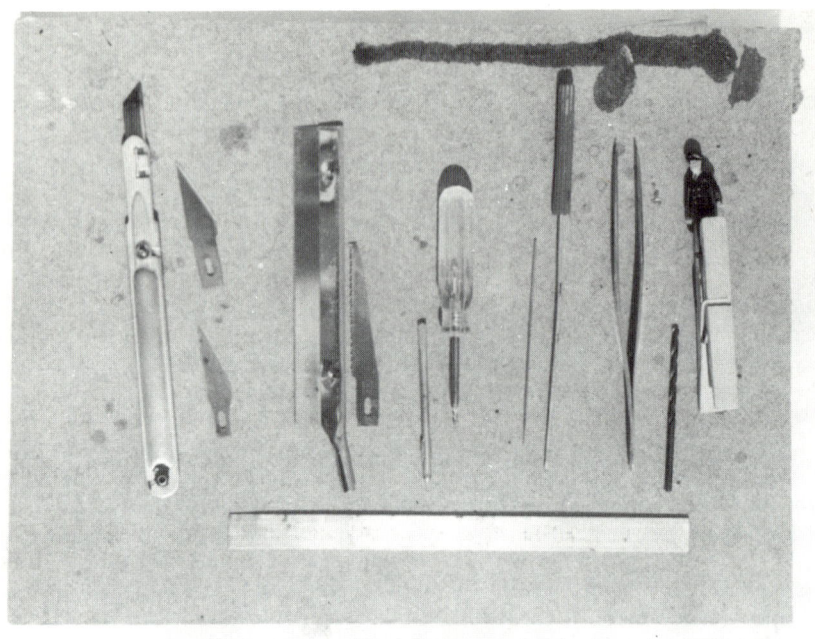

Some basic tools suitable for model soldier work. Left to right: craft knife with spare blades; razor saw blade with alternative small toothed saw blade for craft knife; engraver and scriber; large and small 'mouse tail' files; tweezers; small drill; clothes-peg (holding figure); steel rule (at bottom). All are laid out on a hardboard work surface with glue spillage, etc, already in evidence.

place while the cement dries. Prefer the type with pointed slender ends, if only because you'll most often need to work in fairly restricted areas and the broad-ended type cannot always get where you need to be.

Going on beyond these bare essentials, aim to get the following:

(4) Razor-saw or razor-saw blade.
(5) Pin-chuck and needle drill(s).
(6) Pointed scriber(s) or engraving tools.
(7) Set-square and steel rule.
(8) Small pliers.
(9) Small scissors.

Of the above, the razor-saw becomes important if you get involved in conversion work. It cuts finely and efficiently — ideal for removing a model head or arm when re-aminating, and for dozens of other tasks. With plastic and soft metals, a handle is not always necessary for the razor-saw; it can be held by the metal stub which fits into the handle and still gives sufficient purchase. The heavy duty knife handle takes a razor-saw blade in many cases, and at least one maker (Multicraft) has a small toothed blade about the size of a knife blade which makes a substitute for a razor-saw. The best razor-saw for many years has been that made by X-acto. Conversion work often entails some drilling and you may well need to drill small holes as anchor points, say for helmet plumes, or aigulettes. The pin chuck is like a small screw-driver handle to hold a small pin drill for hand working. In plastics and soft metals this is quite adequate, and, indeed, you can drill quite satisfactorily by rotating the drill only between thumb and forefinger and dispensing with the chuck completely, another tip for the economy-conscious modeller. The pointed scriber can take the form of almost anything with a fine sharp or edged point though proper engraving tools can be purchased if desired; a scriber might be used for any creative task like etching in additional creases on a sleeve, opening up the moulded lips to make a plastic man 'shout', etching in additional hair, making good a seam line over a join in plastic parts, and so on. Pins, beaten out nails, compass points, and so forth can be used as scribers, and a favoured item is a selection of old dental tools (if you have a friendly local dentist). It is absolutely essential, of course, that whatever you use for scribing should have a handle good enough for you to have complete control over the task in hand.

Items 7, 8, and 9 in the list are self-explanatory and you probably have them available already.

With all the above, you are well set up, but there are obviously some 'luxury' items which are handy to have but in no way essential. Among these are:

A small soldering iron of the Weller type.
A small power drill of the Petite type.
A jewellers or toolmaker's vice, such as a Minivice.
D-clamps of the smallest size.
A magnifying glass on a stand or support (there are varieties at varying prices for both stamp collectors and jewellers).

Of the above, the magnifying glass stand and the vice are probably the

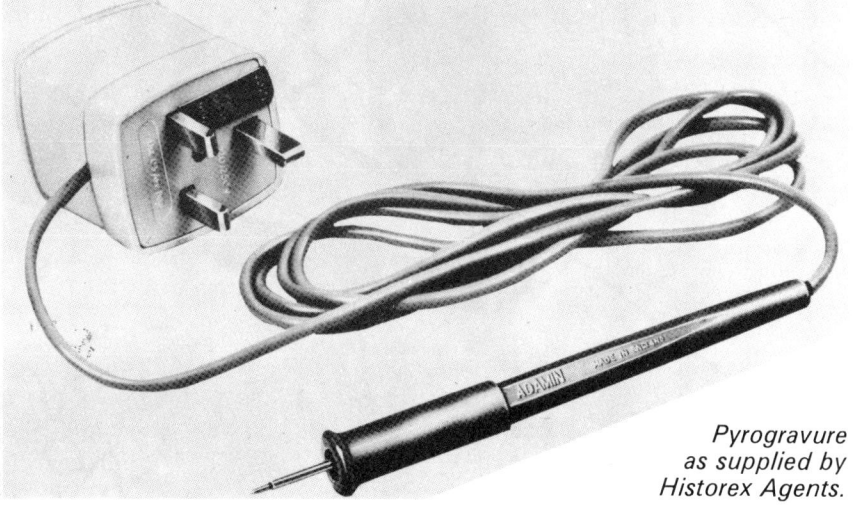

Pyrogravure
as supplied by
Historex Agents.

most useful. You can make model soldiers without ever having to solder; and a power drill, while attractive and usually offered with polishing and grinding heads as well as drills, is relatively rarely needed. In some conversion work the D-clamp is handy, but sprung clothes-pegs or binding with adhesive tape or elastic bands can often be a cheaper substitute.

One last item of interest to the modeller who concentrates on hard plastic figures is the Pyrogravure which Historex market and commend for conversion work with their kits. This amounts to an electrically heated needle working off the mains, It melts the plastic surface to which it is (gently) applied, so that with judicious working the moulded facial features of a plastic man, for example, can be changed — his cheeks, sunken, his brows raised, his hair dishevelled and so on. The mane or tail of a horse can be changed considerably, and buttons and creases can be re-worked on tunics. While in no way necessary, many of the top modellers use a Pyrogravure to create exhibition-standard conversions of Historex and other hard plastic figures.

Keep your tools in an old tin box or wood cigar box, both for safety and neatness. It only remains to say that a good working surface is just as vital as an adequate set of tools. Making a model soldier does not require much space. Some modellers have an old tea-tray with a rim, and this is useful, for everything can stay on the tray at the end of a model session. It also enables you to work on simple kit assembly in an armchair. For conversion work you need to place the tray on a firmer surface, like the kitchen table if you have no special workroom or den. As an alternative to a tray, you'll need a good wood board (say an old drawing board) or a Formica-clad piece of a chipboard — anything that gives a safe, smooth, flat cutting surface.

Finally, for the modeller with the money to spare, it is worth pointing out that comprehensive tool sets in boxes can be had at varying prices. Multicraft and X-acto offer good sets.

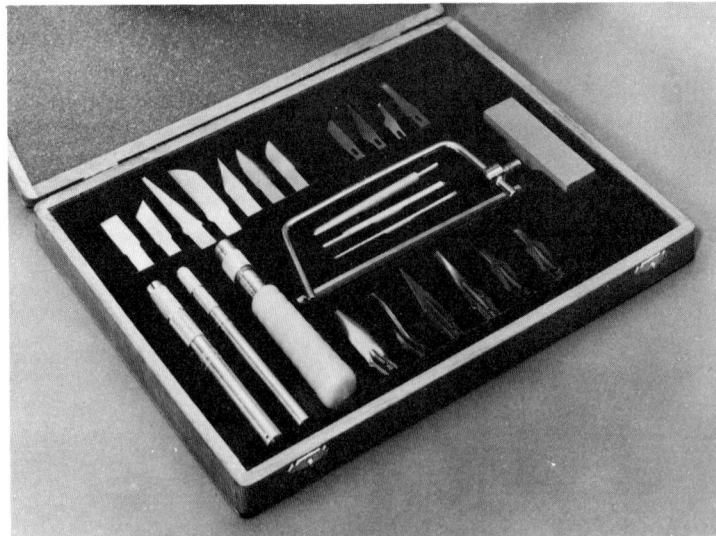

Typical full tool set, in wood case.

5: Materials and Adhesives

THERE are no fixed rules about what materials can be used in model soldier work. You can literally use anything to hand which seems suitable for a specific job, if converting and detailing are your main areas of activity. Thus there are many old 'traditional' items which can be utilised, plus several new ones available on the general model market.

Quality writing paper, card, gummed parcel tape, balsa wood, strip wood, gift-wrapping tape, and veneers are simple materials, easy to obtain, and easy to work. You might use thick paper, for instance, to make a saddle blanket for a miniature horse, or gummed parcel tape in strips for a soldier's cross-belts. There is nothing like wood for depicting wood in miniature; so if you model a soldier carrying wood stakes, the stakes can be cut from slivers of balsa wood. Most applications of these materials are obvious, but as a matter of fact some experienced modellers do some very drastic work with nothing more than paper. Some memorable Afrika Korps figures in the desert winter of 1942-43 were modelled by John Sandars all wearing greatcoats over their tropical gear; the figures were basic Airfix polythene pieces all clothed in greatcoats and mufflers made from paper.

Going on to more complicated materials, brass or copper shim can be used to make items of outer clothing (like cloaks or kilts) and many modellers use the very thin sheet metal which can be obtained from empty tooth-paste tubes. This is very malleable and easy to work. Foil paper is also favoured by some. Other common materials for which you can often find a use include pins, fuse wire or florist's wire, soft copper wire, and the plastic insulation from electrical flex.

Specifically intended for all modellers is that versatile material variously called plastic card, Plastikard, Polycard, or Rikocard, these latter being trade names. Looking like ordinary smooth card, this material joins with plastic cement and has most of the properties of polystyrene. Plastic card can be cut with a craft knife (it will snap through if cut and bent along a straight edge), can be bent and formed by hand in a limited way, and more permanently bent and shaped round formers, being set by plunging into hot water. Thicknesses range from .125 mm to 1.5 mm or even more, depending on the maker and the sheet size similarly varies, but price per sheet is in the 'pocket money' class so that a selection of thicknesses can be purchased quite cheaply. Black and white are the commonest colours, and suitable for most purposes, but some makers offer other colours like red, yellow, green, and blue, which can be useful to the military modeller.

The range of uses for plastic card is enormous; when making model figures you would find the thickest type excellent for making bases either for an individual plastic figure or for a group; items of equipment like haversacks and pouches can be fashioned from plastic card to make up braces and cross-belts; and some modellers have made up strong but effective 'interior' dioramas representing a room, etc, by making an open-sided box entirely from sheets of plastic card; display plinths can be made the same way. Allied to plastic card is the material sold as Microstrip or Ministrip which consists of finely sliced strips of plastic card in varying strip widths from .5 mm wide to 2 mm wide. A selection of these in differing widths or thicknesses is always useful. The virtue of these plastic card items is that the material is extremely strong and adaptable, easy to work and easy to cement, using the same adhesives as you need to work on a plastic kit. Several layers may be laminated together if an extreme thickness is required.

The sprue or runner left over from plastic kits can be handy — such items as water bottles, bedrolls, and the like can be carved from sprue, and sprue stretched over a candle flame can be used for fine details like bayonets or sword blades.

In addition to these important materials, always be on the look out for items which may solve the problem of difficult modelling tasks. One product which came to light in this way was the self-adhesive strip called Chartpak which is sold for draughtsman and designers. It is, in essence, very thinly cut adhesive tape supplied in rolls and very useful for making up harness straps and cross-belts. Airfix and Historex supply a very thin plastic 'ribbon' which is intended itself to be cut into thin strips to make harness and belts of scale thickness; this comes with the kits and it is well worth keeping any left over from an assembled kit. Gift-wrapping tape makes an admirable substitute in many ways superior.

Which leads us on to stress the importance of looking out for, and keeping, any likely looking scrap items or spare parts which might conceivably find a later use in conversion or detailing work. Any parts left over from kit assembly or conversion work should be carefully kept as a matter of course. For example, a water bottle or pack not used on one figure can be used on another. Most of the plastic kit producers, and some of those in the metal kit business as well, supply optional parts within the kit, so you'll be left with some of these. The Historex and Segom importers in Great Britain, if not always elsewhere, offer a fine mail order service of spare parts and is possible to make up figures entirely from scratch simply by judicious ordering of the necessary legs, bodies, arms, heads, and other parts. The keen converter should obtain the lists from the importers and see just what is to be had in this way. Several of the metal figure makers, notably Rose, have offered spare heads and other parts for many years and the model figure enthusiast is well served in this direction, at least as far as 54 mm scale goes. As mentioned in

    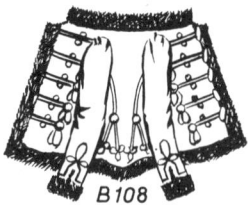

B109   B110   B111   B106   B108

Typical components available separately from Rose Models and shown in their extensive catalogue (courtesy Rose Models).

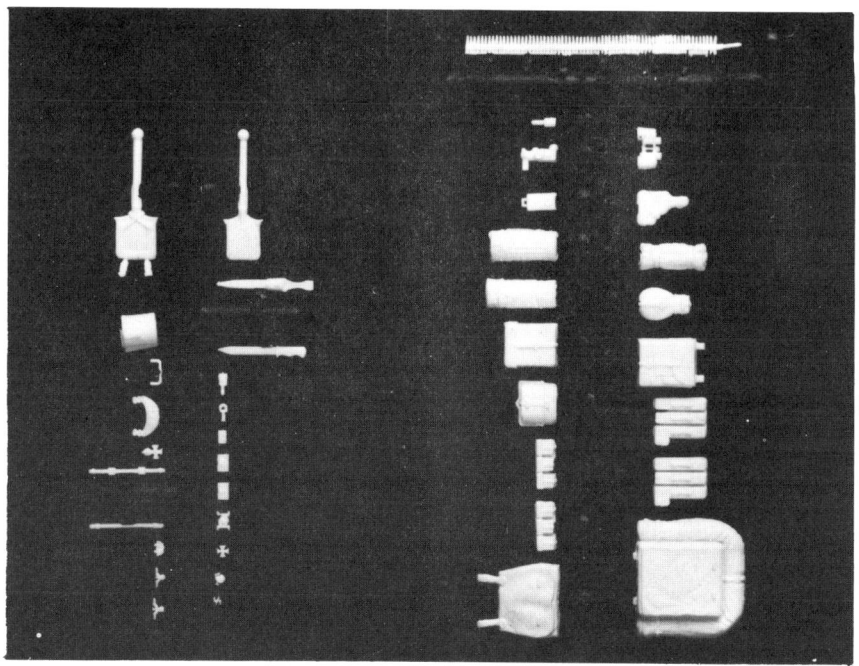

Armour Accessories set of German infantry equipment, 54 mm scale, specifically intended for conversion work and moulded in polystyrene.

an earlier chapter, items intended for other modelling activities can also be of great use. The model farm and model rail accessory field are specially fruitful. A packing case intended for a model train load can equally well serve as an ammunition box for a model soldier to carry in a diorama, and so on. The imaginative modeller will keep an eye open for any such suitable material; on some occasions even trinkets from Christmas crackers or plastic items (like stoppers) from domestic packaging have proved useful for conversion or diorama work. Let nothing pass you by.

Some clear plastic boxes, which are easy enough to find these days, make admirable storage receptacles for spare parts and useful pieces. The 'see through' box obviates the need for rummaging through to look for suitable items. 'Bulk' materials like card, cartridge paper, plastic card, and so on, can be kept in a shallow cardboard box or an old shoe-box — get more boxes if your stock increases — labelled accordingly. Storage of bits and pieces, plus tools, paints, and adhesives, is often overlooked in the first flush of modelling enthusiasm, but it is an important matter for not only does it obviate loss or 'wandering' of key items but it helps to make your hobby more domestically acceptable if the associated paraphernalia is kept tidy.

Adhesives

Most general modelling these days calls for certain basic adhesives and those most necessary for model soldier work are as follows:

Plastic cement: Most plastic kit makers sell their own brands, and the material is widely sold in tube form at hobby shops and other stores. It is used for joining all kit materials that are in polystyrene (hard) plastic and works by dissolving the plastic at the point of application, so in effect 'welding' the plastic parts together. It must be used with care as too much will squeeze out of the join and mark the area adjacent to the join. Drops split on to a plastic surface will mark it, and trying to remove spilt cement from plastic while it is still wet will merely compound the problem. With model figures careful use is of great importance, since the detail moulded in, which might include cloth texture, is of the finest type which can easily be ruined. Some brands have a tendency to 'string' and the 'strings' can sometimes add themselves, unnoticed until too late, to the figure's surface. Application of the cement direct from the nozzle is not commended, and a match-stalk or wood cocktail stick makes a good applicator, taking a suitably sized blob of cement from the nozzle of the tube. If sparingly applied, the little cement which may squeeze from the join, say when limb halves are cemented together, should be left to harden. Careful rubbing down when the parts are set hard will then probably eliminate the join line, since the tiny amount of excess cement will have acted as its own 'filler'. Plastic cement is also sold under the name of 'polystyrene cement'.

Liquid Plastic Cement/Mek-Pak: A liquid cement which also joins polystyrene is sold under various brand-names. It varies slightly in its properties, one brand from another, but essentially it works like plastic cement but in a more delicate manner, due to its watery nature. This cement comes in bottles and is applied with a tip of a brush, the procedure being to hold the parts together, then run a brushful of cement round the join. The cement runs into the join, and by surface tension runs into those parts which the brush cannot necessarily reach. The advantage is that any spillage on to the adjacent surfaces, if indeed there is any, does not usually make such a prominent mark since it does not eat so deeply into a surface. Many modellers use plastic cement for assembly of the main parts of a figure, then utilise the Mek-Pak when it comes to adding the tiny details. In a Historex kit, for instance, many buttons and badges come as the most minute separate mouldings which could easily dissolve completely if stuck with plastic cement. The better alternative is to hold the tiny part in its precise position either with tweezers or a pin, then secure it with a touch of a brush loaded with Mek-Pak. Points to remember with this type of cement is that it gives off fairly pungent fumes and evaporates quite fast. So keep the bottle sealed except when actually in use (this also reduces the chance of knocking it over), and work in well ventilated surroundings. Brushes need washing out in brush cleaner after use or they will solidify and become useless. It is best to keep a brush specially for cementing rather than risk ruining a good paint brush.

ABS cement: This is another type of cement sold specifically for joining components in structural kits made of hard ABS plastic (whose properties differ slightly from polystyrene), such as those made by Plastruct. Figures made in ABS are rare but may be encountered.

PVC cement: This is sold by Humbrol (and other makers) mainly for domestic repair work, since many household goods are of PVC these days. If you convert modern Britain's plastic figures, however, and make Helmet kits, PVC is the plastic mainly in use and the appropriate cement is useful, even though Five-Minute Epoxy can be used successfully on PVC models.

Universal Adhesive: This is widely sold under various brand-names of which Uhu is probably the best known. It is a fairly good universal adhesive which can be used to assemble cast metal kits, and cements general materials like card and wood. It dries transparent which can be an advantage and can be used on polythene figures if the joint is reinforced by pins or wire. Other than following the maker's instructions in application, and avoiding an excess on a join, its use is straightforward. A tube is always a handy investment.

Five-Minute Epoxy: This fairly recent development in glues has to some extent ousted 'universal' type glues from the modeller's inventory. There are several brands, including Devcon and Britfix 19. Essentially this comes in a twin-pack, one tube containing the adhesive itself, and the other a hardener. Equal quantities are mixed together on a piece of old card, the two surfaces to be joined are thinly but evenly coated, then pressed firmly together. After five minutes the cemented parts are firmly enough set to be handled, and the join is of a permanent nature subject to the usual care in handling any model. The great advantage of this adhesive is its ease of handling, its speed of setting, and, most important of all, the fact that it allows materials which are normally thought of as non-compatible to be cemented together at will. Thus polythene parts, for many years extremely difficult to cement together, can now be satisfactorily glued (at least for model soldier conversion purposes), metal parts may be glued to plastic parts, and so. The original long setting Epoxy resin cements may be used, of course, but the 'Five-Minute' variety is the type most useful to modellers and no scale figure enthusiast should be without it.

ACC Cement: Most recent development of all is a 'wonder' cement called alpha cyanoacrylate which, though by no means essential, will be of value to the prolific advanced modeller. ACC is a bonding cement which joins on contact and is specially useful for joining metal parts, or normally non-compatible parts like metal and plastic. There are various trade names including IS-12, Aron Alpha, and Kodak 910, and it is mainly intended for industrial use. The properties of this cement can be unfriendly, indeed dangerous, when it is not carefully used. It can fume, bonds on contact, 'creeps' by capillary action, and must be used sparingly. The best way of application is to hold the parts to be joined exactly in position — say an arm to a shoulder, or a holster to a belt — then apply just a drop of ACC by pin point to the join. Capillary action will do the rest and the parts will be instantly bonded. It is essential not to get ACC on your fingers — the metal part can be cemented permanently to your finger, or two finger tips can be cemented together and only the painful process of slicing through the skin will separate them! We cannot advise the use of this cement for anyone other than very experienced adult modellers, and it must, of course, be kept well away from children.

While there are other adhesives available — wood glues, Seccotine, PVA 'White' glue, paste, etc, which may be used in general model work, and may be required for scenic or display work (for instance to make a wood plinth), the adhesives described here are those most essential for actual model soldier work.

Fillers

Whether or not you need to use fillers rather depends on how deeply involved you get in conversion work. You can build up a good collection without the need for extensive remodelling. However, for the sort of conversions which attract keen modellers the availability of plastic materials now makes it possible to carry out ambitious work. Among useful items are:

Plastic Putty: Also known as 'Customising Body Putty', this amounts to a finely textured putty which sets hard with an appearance like polystyrene and can then by filed, sanded, and carved like polystyrene plastic. It should be applied in thin layers with a spatula (an old screw driver of small size is ideal) as it contracts slightly on setting, and large areas are best built up a little at a time. As it is porous to a degree, it needs an separate undercoat before the figure as a whole is undercoated — otherwise paint may be absorbed, and the puttied area will be only too obvious. Humbrol, AMT, and a similar material, Green Stuff, are the commonest brands. Most modellers prefer Green Stuff.

Isopon, Milliput, Plastic Padding: Those are all materials sold mainly by motor accessory and hardware stores and originally intended for car body and household repair work. In essence these are epoxy type substances which are 'cured' and then harden to a rock-like texture. There are yet other brands with similar properties. They allow very large areas to be built up, then carved, sanded, or filed into various shapes. Milliput and Plastic Padding are the easiest to use, though fairly slow setting, and they 'take' on hard plastic. Smooth plastic needs roughening slightly to help 'key' it to the material. Isopon has slightly different properties. Though it will not adhere to plastic, it hardens more quickly and can be used over wire 'armature' frameworks to build up what amounts to a complete figure. One of the leading converters, Roy Dilley, often fashions cloaks, etc , from paper over a basic metal figure, then coats the paper in Isopon so it sets rigid. Arthur Woolford is a leading exponent of the use of Isopon and has a large collection of 54 mm figures made from this material over wire. A good deal of practice and experimentation is necessary to work out techniques, but obviously the use of these proprietary plastics has limitless possibilities for ambitious modelling.

'Home-made' Putty: Some modellers have made an effective type of plastic putty by slicing up the sprues or runners from plastic kits, dropping the thin slices into a bottle of liquid cement, and waiting for the plastic to dissolve, so forming a putty-like substance which can be applied by spatula as previously described. The consistency can be varied by adding more or less sliced plastic according to needs.

Surface Coverings

Paints are dealt with a separate chapter, but there are two key substances which are again of fairly recent origin but most useful to figure modellers.

Unibond: This is a milky PVA substance (actually an adhesive) which is sold in tubes or plastic bottles and dries to give a hard transparent skin. Its great value is with polythene or other soft plastic figures on which normal

Conversions of Britain's Deetail figures in PVC by Roy Dilley show the Unibond covering prior to painting. These are American Civil War soldiers with new heads and details to make RN personnel of 1900 for a Gardner gun diorama.

model paints will not successfully 'take'. On these figures, when painted with normal plastic enamels, there was always a tendency for the paint to rub off even with the most careful handling. A thorough coating of Unibond dries hard and gives the modeller a painting surface which can then be treated just like hard plastic and painted directly. Elmers White Glue is an equivalent American brand. In theory you could water down the stiffer type of PVA white glues and use them, but we have achieved foolproof results with the brands named here.

Polyurethane Varnish: Many metal figures have in the past been ruined over a period of years by 'lead disease' — the oxidisation of the lead content of the figure. This manifests itself as a white fungus-like development which ruins the paintwork and in extreme cases leads to the entire figure crumbling away. Polyurethane varnish is now recommended for covering all metal figures (or those featuring any metal parts), working the varnish well into every nook and cranny so that no part is left uncovered. This forms a damp-proof, air-proof skin over the entire figure and should preserve it indefinitely. Use *matt* varnish and ensure it is rock hard before attempting any further paint work. It may now be purchased in small tinlets (eg, by Joy brand), convenient for modellers.

6: Information and Research

ONE of the great features of any constructive hobby is the way that it opens the door to all sorts of new knowledge. In furthering your hobby you cannot help but pick up a good deal of passing information, and with model soldiers you can make an acquaintance with history in a particularly vivid way for you are creating in a miniature form some of the very people — the soldiers—who made history through the great battles and campaigns in which they fought.

We are all gifted with a degree of imagination and, indeed, anyone who has purchased some model soldiers and then, perhaps, gone on to buy a book on the subject has done so because, consciously or not, the model soldiers have caught his imagination. Any type of modelling exercises the imagination, and once you are interested in model soldiers you use it in full measure; the very process of animating a figure or arranging a diorama demands that you give it a lot of thought to arrive at a successful model. But to feed your imagination you need more than the raw materials — the tools, the paints, the kit of parts, or the box of soldiers — you also need the background information, or the means of finding it, to make sure that your model is an accurate as you can get it and that its full potential is realised.

Very often, of course, the kit maker or figure maker gives you some basic information and/or diagrams which give a brief amount of information relevant to the figure(s) in hand; but again some cast figures are sold with no accompanying literature, some items are sold ready-painted, and yet others are sold with a wealth of supplementary information even including colour plates! Obviously the commercial figure maker has to do the necessary research to develop and produce the basic model, but there is big variation in what he then passes on to the purchaser in the form of assembly and colouring instructions. And again, study of what a kit or model maker might say in the instruction sheet can reveal discrepancies when set against other authorities. So it is clearly very useful to be able to check and amplify the information which comes with the kit in order that there be no doubt about the detailing and painting of the model. When it comes to a figure you have converted from another, you may be entirely on your own. You decide what figure you want to make, you find the source of parts for the conversion work, and all the information needed for the painting. Without all the necessary information you cannot really begin; no good, for instance, starting to make a new figure if you don't know the cut of the tunic.

More than any other type of model, the scale figure offers traps for the unwary. There are endless small points of detail — lace and buttons on the tunic, variations in shoulder straps, different orders of dress, tiny changes which depend on the year being depicted, and subtle changes in uniform colour. The audience for your figures will often well-informed enthusiasts

Books, postcards, cuttings, magazines, and printed ephemera of many kinds can be used as a source of model research. Here are some typical items.

themselves and will cast an eagle eye over your work, but even if nobody else sees your models you will want the satisfaction of knowing that they are as accurate as you can get them. Examples of 'howlers' in model work with scale figures can be seen in abundance, even in published articles.

The release of a new German self-propelled gun made in kit form by a major manufacturer occasioned some comment when the display model appeared with the gun commander wearing a completely scarlet cap; on investigation it transpired that the modeller who assembled and painted the prototype kit had seen an arrow on the painting sketch pointing to the cap and marked 'Red'. Some study and knowledge of the subject would show that the red refers to the Waffenfarbe (arm of service) piping round the rim of the cap, and not the entire cap, which would have been field grey, of course. Another example concerns a high quality cast metal 'collectors' figure in a specialist retailer's window, offered as a ready-painted item at a high price; the figure was a German Waffen-SS machine gunner, supposedly in black parade uniform and beautifully finished. This was very fine except that the actual uniform in which the figure is cast was only ever issued as field grey service dress. This particular example shows that even the customer who had not done his 'homework' on the uniform could well find himself paying out a high sum of money for a completely inaccurate piece. These examples are taken almost at random, but show how inadequate research can be a definite pitfall, spoiling a lot of otherwise excellent work.

So we have established that before you rush too far into the art of model soldier making you need to start finding our information relevant to what you are working on. Fortunately, in recent years, the amount of available information has grown vastly, with a great output of books and magazine articles. Among the published material you are likely to find something on the periods and forces which particularly interest you. Such eras as the Napoleonic Wars, the British and American Civil Wars, and the two World Wars are particularly well-covered in print, but some digging around will reveal information on many other periods.

As with figures, so with books and journals. Your personal budget may be generous enough for you to purchase a vast home library of publications so that you have to hand all that you need; but you may be able to afford very little, in which case join your local public library where you can borrow books you may not be able to buy for yourself. There are now so many books on military uniforms either currently or recently in print that a list would fill this book alone; however, as basic books which cover military uniforms very broadly it would well be worth anyone's while purchasing the following:

Kannik, *Military Uniforms in Colour* (Blandford) (Macmillan, USA).
Funcken, *Le Costume et Les Armes Des Soldats de Tous les Temps* (Castermann) (also published in an English language edition as *Armies and Uniforms* by Ward Lock—two volumes).

The above publishers also produce other uniform books dealing with specific periods in more detail, Castermann in particular having fine volumes covering the Napoleonic Wars and the two World Wars. However, the titles mentioned are ideal for beginners for they pack many colour illustrations and much basic information into what are good value books.

Aside from any uniform books you buy yourself or obtain via a lending library, there are very many more books which provide regimental histories or background histories to battles and campaigns of every period. Indeed, it is when you move on to these in the search for supplementary information, that your imagination may really be stimulated, for in no time at all you start to absorb the very atmosphere of the times. This is not to be sneered at, for a knowledge of the background to what you are modelling is very valuable. Your model figure is more than just a 'clothes-horse' carrying the uniform of a period. You may find that at a particular time, the regiment you are portraying in model form was a raggle-taggle bunch of defeated wretches, and this may then be reflected in the way your model is completed, with torn, dirty clothes, and unkempt hair and appearance.

One essential item which costs little enough is a notebook in which the results of any research can be recorded. Notes and sketches can be made, not only for figures you may be working on currently but also for any models you may have in mind for longer term projects. Record the source of any book or article from which notes are taken, so that you can return to the source without too much trouble later on, if necessary; this is an important consideration if your notes came from a borrowed book. Take the note book in your pocket to any museum, reference library, or exhibition, and use it in general as a running work-book.

You'll find that books apart, magazine articles, old prints, old postcards, cigarette cards, specialist military museums, and modelling society meets can all be rich sources of reference material. Military museums are always worth a visit in the quest for information. Aside from nationally established museums, there are regimental museums in some numbers, often little known, specially so in Great Britain. The book *A Guide to Military Museums* (Bellona/Argus) is an inexpensive buy which lists and locates about 150 of them. Most military museums have libraries, and most societies, such as BMSS, have regular meetings. If you are able to join one of the national or local military modelling clubs, this can be extremely useful for the meetings not only bring you into contact with fellow modellers and top experts, but give a further stimulus to your modelling activities when you see other people's models. Many club meetings also have trade stalls dealing in figures, books, and militaria, while auctions and outings may also be organised from time to time. BMSS, IPMS, and others, such as the Military Historical Society also publish journals for members. Information on the whereabouts and activities of clubs and societies is regularly carried in *Military Modelling* magazine. Second-hand bookshops and junk stalls are a frequent source of old publications or prints and are worth perusal if time permits.

Magazines, especially old back numbers can be very useful. Into this category can be placed very old magazines, such as the *Army & Navy Illustrated* and the German *Signal,* which were packed with choice pictures and are now sought after collectors' items. Modelling magazines, like *Military Modelling,* are a good source of information, and of course, the current issue keeps you in touch with the most recent developments in the hobby. Of particular value are the new kit and book reviews, the model reviews in particular often giving a good assessment of a particular release which may help you decide whether or not to purchase. Also of great use to your own personal research is the popular feature 'Uniforminformation' — if you are completely stumped, write in with your query to *Military Modelling* and the experts will try to find the answer and publish the information.

If your research becomes very extensive and your modelling activities are prolific, then scrapbooks or manila wallets in which cuttings, photostats, prints, postcards, and so on can be filed are a very neat and handy way of keeping the material organised and readily to hand. If you have a camera, bear in mind that some museums allow photography of their exhibits subject to permission being sought, but check up on all aspects of the situation first; for instance flash may not be allowed.

Research can become a very absorbing and interesting pastime in its own right and, indeed, some enthusiasts get so involved in research that actual modelling starts to become a secondary interest and in some cases gets dropped altogether! Military uniforms and equipment, however, form such a vast subject for study and cover such an immense span of time that there is always something new to discover. Even periods of history, such as the Napoleonic Wars and World War 2, which on the surface appear to be well documented, still have an enormous amount to yield up in the way of uniform information. Research to back up a modelling project actually offers any keen scale figure modeller the chance to uncover new facts on uniform details, and to pass it on to others, perhaps, by articles or letters submitted to a magazine, or by a model conversion at a society meeting. Some information comes to light in the most random of ways; even while preparing this book we found an obscure old publication by Lord Baden-Powell, on sale for a few pence in a junk shop, which proved to include sketches and information on the uniform 'BP' evolved for both men and women members of the famous South African Constabulary which he commanded at Mafeking. So keep a good look out all the time for anything which may be useful for research, even when you are not, perhaps, actively pursuing hobby work.

The one thing to remember when doing any sort of research for modelling, however, is not to make a nuisance of yourself. Do not deface borrowed books, infringe copyright, or abuse hospitality. The only other golden rule, especially when researching uniforms, is not to take the first bit of information you find on a uniform as the end of the story. Compare several authorities, note that artist's drawings of centuries ago often conflict in detail, one with the other, or with recorded facts — 'artist's licence' is age-old, and in the old days there were sometimes variations which were perfectly legitimate. The most authoritative of modern books and articles on uniforms usually point out inconsistencies, and are sometimes able to say what is most likely to be authentic. Where this does not happen, you need to be the judge and work out the likeliest answer for yourself. To illustrate the point, there is even divergence of opinion on some details of the Scots Grey uniuniform worn at the Battle of Waterloo — and this particular subject has been researched and recorded more than most.

7: Conversion Potential

HAVING reached the stage, perhaps, where you have been able to decide what sort of model soldiers, and which scale, appeals to you, you are well placed to put some of the theories discussed in the preceding chapters well and truly into practice. Many modellers, indeed, will already be building up collections by the time they come to read this book and will have already made some decisions — which may or may not be influenced by what we have to say.

If you are a complete novice, take some sound advice and keep your projects short and simple at least to start with. Depending on his purse, the average modeller probably dabbles in all types of figure, typically working from the cheaper plastic kits or 'toy' figures if necessary and then spreading his further purchases among the more expensive plastic or metal assembly kits, the cast 'collector' figures and possibly even a ready-painted piece or two. Many work almost entirely at the cheaper end of the market, partly because this makes model soldiers one of the least expensive of hobbies, but also because one has less reluctance to experiment with and convert a model costing only a few pence than with a 'collector' model which involves a considerable outlay. With the exception of ready-painted pieces, virtually all kits or models as purchased have to be finished off either by painting, assembly, extra detailing or a combination of all these. This gives the builder the chance to apply his own touch of individuality to the model, to create something quite distinctive and unique.

Almost any tiny change, even no more than can be carried out by a variation in painting, can constitute a 'conversion' in model soldier parlance, though the term is usually taken to mean some physical change as well. Because magazine articles most often publish very ambitious and complicated conversion articles, catering for the more advanced worker, the beginner might well get the impression that conversion work is beyond his capabilities. However, nothing is further from the truth. You can carry out a lot of very satisfying conversion work with no more than the most minor changes to a model which can, nonetheless, change its character and appearance completely. To take a quite simple example, the familiar Britain's marching Guardsman (either the plastic or modern metal variety) takes on a quite different appearance when his head with the bearskin is changed for a head with a forage cap, as is worn on occasion for drill or guard order. Then repainting the model authentically will further the transformation, and the laymen will not recognise its origin as a cheap 'toy' piece. For further variety even this model can be changed in rank, say to corporal or lance-sergeant, or, by adding a sash, to full sergeant. The head, when changed, can be cemented in the 'eyes right' or 'eyes left' position, and by progressing further still, by changing button, insignia, and facing detail during the painting, any of the footguards regiments can be depicted. By purchasing several of these basic figures a complete marching picquet with sergeant, corporal, and men can be modelled on a suitable diorama base. All these changes can be carried out on one of the

Above: Expert conversion work by Ray Anderson created this US cavalry-man watering his horse, made entirely from Historex plastic components. Pyrogravure was used for the realistic hair effect. Below: Plastic kits allow even a beginner to make simple changes. Mounted infantry man (on left) by Tamiya is shown with the same item made up to vary arm positions, details, and colours.

Another fine 'mini' diorama by Ray Anderson made entirely from Historex spare components, and portraying Indians returning from Little Big Horn. Grass is made from teased out string as described in this book. Bottom of an old table leg forms the plinth in this case. Below: Officers and other ranks of the Rifle Brigade, 1914, made from old Britain's figures by Roy Dilley. Mounted officer is a converted huntsman.

most basic of available 'toy' models and could give you ten or more different end results.

As your modelling skill grows you may want to try re-animating existing figures to give something that looks really different, but before you rush into these more complicated endeavours, take note that there are so many plastic 'toy' figures of good quality to be had these days that it is possible to find some piece, somewhere, in almost any imaginable position, and quite drastic conversions can be carried out with no need to alter the position of the figure; instead, the necessary work concentrates on uniform and equipment detail which is very satisfying and interesting in itself, but the end result alters the figure completely even though it retains exactly the post supplied by the manufacturer. To illustrate this point we show two entirely different conversions from the same basic figure — the well-known Britain's model which is sold as a 'Military Showjumper'. Our two conversions will be familiar to many since they have been published before, but they show how variations on the theme can come up with models depicting entirely different eras. Roy Dilley converted the figure into a trooper of the 10th Hussars in foreign service dress 1879; the original horse was used, the rider's head was changed for a Rose cast metal head of the appropriate type, and this was glued in place glancing to the right; all the equipment was fashioned and added from spare parts. as were uniform and saddle details after which the work was painted. Chris Ellis converted the same basic item to a Waffen-SS cavalry despatch rider of 1942; in this case Tamiya plastic head, helmet, and equipment was used, the sleeve cuffs were reshaped to depict an elasticated combat smock, and the man was mounted on a different Britain's horse. In neither case was any attempt made to change the positions of either man or horse, and both modellers were following the rule of not introducing any unnecessary complications into good basic material — the 'keep it simple' theme emphasised at the start of this chapter.

Endless further examples could be cited. Here are a few: good basic British World War I figures in 54 mm scale can be made from Airfix or Britain's Japanese troops with the heads removed and replaced, and all equipment changed as necessary — there are so many different poses in these sets that only a glutton for punishment would really need to try the more complicated work involved in re-animating them. German World War I troops can be made the same way from both maker's sets, the added complication here being that the patch pockets must be carved from all the figures (though this is a simple enough job), but there is no need to change the heads in this case. Re-detailing nearly all the available Britain's Deetail and Airfix 54 mm figures merely as they come, added to the task of repainting them, would give any modeller virtually a life-time of cheap and simple projects at rock bottom prices, and in most cases the poses as supplied are so good that it is difficult to improve on them.

Obviously, the average modeller tends to be selective and in practice is not likely to slavishly restrict himself to a particular range just because it is cheap. The enthusiast for models of the Napoleonic era might for instance work up inexpensive pieces from the Britain's Deetail figures, the Airfix polythene figures, the Airfix polystyrene kits, Helmet kits, Historex kits, Segom parts,

Top: Waffen-SS mounted despatch rider of 1942 made by Chris Ellis from the Britain's 'Military Showjumper'. Above: 10th Hussar of 1879 made by Roy Dilley from the same figure, using the original horse. Basic figure as purchased stands on the right. Below: Simplest of conversions. Britain's Deetail American Civil War figure on right made into a British Infantryman of 1898, with new Rose cast metal head and detail changes, including gaiters.

and metal kits or figures. In every popular period, such as World War 2 and the Napoleonic Wars, there is a truly vast choice and it becomes a very useful skill to be able to look at all commercially available figures in any price range and assess their suitability for a place in your own collection. You may be looking for a particular regiment or unit, or a figure in a particular position, or a combination of the two.

Look at a figure for its conversion potential. Is the pose and basic dress suitable if the equipment details are changed? Is the pose just what you need, even though the dress is completely wrong and will need major re-styling? Is the figure just right save for its pose—and if so does it look an easy matter to reposition the limbs? These are the sorts of question you need to meditate over in the judicious selection of figures for your collection. Here are a few random examples. To build up your collection of Third Reich figures you need a Political Leader in every-day dress; maybe no firm makes a model sold under this title, but a glance at the uniformed Britain's 'Zoo Keeper' figure shows that only minor details and a repaint will give you what you need. Roy Dilley made farriers of both the British and German Armies by using the old metal Britain's 'Blacksmith' figure (now discontinued) and changing the head. And many modellers have made crouching gunners or mechanics servicing vehicles in diorama scenes by utilising the various mechanics made as electric slot-racing accessories.

When it comes to more ambitious poses, it may not be possible to find any commercial figure which meets requirements. Such situations as the act of mounting a horse, jumping out of a vehicle, a man falling injured, or pitching over a horse's head are quite rarely modelled commercially. Similarly, a large diorama depicting some famous military action may require a multitude of differing poses quite beyond the relatively few available in any kit or model range. It is in this sort of situation that the ingenuity and imagination of the modeller is called into full play. Existing figures must be studied closely to see what parts can be utilised, and the immense value of having a collection of spare parts is realised. A good deal of 'armchair' work can be absorbing here, for with some assorted kits, figures, and spare parts you can sit down and work out permutations which might give the figure you want. As firms like Historex and Segom sell spare components separately, you can select likely sounding pieces from their lists if you do not actually have them to hand. Norman Abbey and Ray Anderson are two leading exponents of the art of making up completely new figures from appropriate Historex and Segom parts, and examples of their work are illustrated in this book. The availability of these parts is a boon to modellers, but they do not exhaust the possibilities. The component parts of Tamiya and Airfix kits can be cross-matched in a similar way; for instance we wanted a motor-cyclist in tropical dress (Afrika Korps) to replace the overcoated figure in the well-known Tamiya German BMW 1:35 scale motor-cycle kit. The answer was found in the Tamiya set of Afrika Korps figures, and it proved possible to use the legs of the running figure from the latter kit together with a torso and arms from other figures in the set to give a seated rider in tropical trousers and shirt; similar adaptation gave other suitable figures to enable the complete BMW combination to take

Above: Norman Abbey made all the US Cavalry figures in this fine diorama from Segom plastic components altered to suit. Below: French Foreign Legion men of 1939, converted from Airfix 54 mm polythene figures by John Sandars.

its place in a Western Desert diorama. Plastic putty and other modelling materials must be used as well, of course, in this sort of project.

Aside from the art of building up figures from kit parts to give an entirely new looking piece, there are similar possibilities with larger chunks of figure being transposed. Typically this involves cutting through the waist of two figures, and mating the lower torso and legs of one with the upper torso of the other. Providing the two parts are in correct proportion to each other, you can end up with a figure which looks entirely original, particularly if uniform and equipment details are also changed.

Re-positioning of limbs may be required in any kind of conversion from the simplest to the most complicated. This can involve changing the angle of a bent arm or leg by partially cutting through, and using a putty filler and cement, or it can involve complete removal of a limb at the shoulder or thigh, either replacing it with a new limb, or altering the angle and position of the original limb before replacing it.

Any of these tasks are simple enough in themselves, using the appropriate tools, but a further consideration which must also be made concerns the appearance of the outer clothing. For when the position of any real figure changes, so does the fit of the outer clothing relative to the body inside. This must be reflected in any model figure too.

Fortunately this self-evident fact can be examined at first hand. Bend your own arm and note how creases and folds form on the inside of the sleeve; straighten your arm and these folds will disappear, but new longer ones may form from the shoulder. Similar changes will be noted for any position taken up by a clothed body. When working on a scale conversion, therefore, this fact must be remembered. A good model has the folds and creases realistically depicted; if not then, for example, cut through the elbow to straighten the arm, remember to file off or carve away the elbow folds, and if necessary carve or etch in new ones in the appropriate positions. In an unclothed body the changes may be less obvious in model form, but note that in a typical situation the muscle formation of, say, a native warrior, will be affected by his action (eg, arm raised to throw a spear, or legs braced while repelling an attack).

Observation and study of real figures, either human or animal, can be of great assistance in the appreciation of how the body form changes in varying positions, and how clothing 'sits' on the body relative to its position. The very simplest modelling aid when carrying out animation and conversion work is yourself (or a co-operative friend) and a long mirror. Wearing clothing roughly equivalent to the model in hand (eg, jacket and trousers, the latter tucked into your socks, for a typical infantryman), take up the position of the figure (use a broomstock for a rifle) and see just how creases and folds form in the clothing. Make allowance, if necessary, for other factors like long gaiters, belts, and packs which may add to the constriction of the clothing. Add to this any pictorial evidence from your research work and there should be no problems in visualising the appearance. It is hardly necessary to be a student of anatomy in order to be a successful model converter, but there are a number of art books to be had in libraries (of the 'How to draw the Human Figure', and 'How to draw Horses' variety) which well repay study for

These are not finished dioramas, but they show the adaptability of typical 'action pose' figures to many different groupings and situations. Above: The complete set of German Panzer Grenadiers by Tamiya takes cover behind a tank. Below: Three different groupings (walls, sandbags, barrels) each of which could be used on a 'mini' diorama base with suitable scenic ground treatment. Accessory items are also from Tamiya. Try out grouping situations like this when working out dioramas.

Above: Very effective diorama using model trees (Britain's), Polyfilla, scenic coverings, and farm accessories (sacks and crates). Figures are Britain's conversions in 54 mm by Roy Dilley. Below: Old Guard 54 mm Waffen-SS machine gun team on a typical 'mini' diorama base. The wood plinth is neatly varnished and titled, while plaster, flock powder, and farmyard walling are used for scenic work.

WAFFEN SS DIVISION "DAS REICH"

they deal with questions of proportions and muscle formation. Also commended is study of the books *The Human Form in Motion* and *Animals in Motion* by Edweard Muybridge (Dover Publications, New York) or any of several recent books on the work of Muybridge; he was a pioneer of stop-motion photography and photographed humans and animals in long picture sequences carrying out typical activities such as running, walking, climbing, etc. If funds run to such luxury, Roy Dilley commends the purchase of an artist's 'mannikin' figure, the jointed representational dummy sold in art shops which can be set in any desired position.

While the foregoing deals with practicalities, it is clearly of little use to set off converting or animating a figure if you are not clear from the start on what you hope to achieve as an end result. Aimless modelling not only leads to poor and characterless results, with consequent dissatisfaction, but also fails to exploit your imaginative faculties. Some pre-planning can save both time and frustration later. Roy Dilley has long postulated the 'five W' rule for pre-planning so that every figure you make can be related to an overall modelling objective. In summary the 'five Ws' are: Who?, Where?, When?, What?, Why?

Who? Determine the figure's rank, regiment, and personality. Is he an officer, a sergeant, a recruit, or an actual person, such as a famous general or character from military history. Establish at this time all the facts of uniform and clothing, insignia, etc, relative to the selected figure and seek out reference material.

Where? Determine the situation — in a battle, on guard, walking-out, suiting an existing diorama, etc — which will in turn effect the required position or animation.

What? Determine what the figure will be doing and how armed or equipped for the task.

When? This is allied to the above, in that a precise time and date is imagined and then related to the real situation at the time. An actual date can greatly affect the finished appearance of the model. For instance taking a British Coldstream Guardsman at Waterloo (or a diorama featuring several Guardsmen) you might decide that the defence of Hougoumont was to be the theme, in which case the stress of battle would be a very necessary consideration to be reflected in the finish of the model. The same figure placed vaguely in an 'on guard, 1815 period' theme might look very different, smart, well turned out and under no great stress. Your research material will help to establish the 'when' factor.

Why? This relates to the actual situation of the individual figure. He may be now established as a private of the Coldstream Guards, in 1815, at the defence of Hougoumont. Why is he there? Defending the walls or gate perhaps, so he probably won't be wearing his full pack, and possibly his shako has been knocked off too.

Taking this one example it can be seen that the well-known Airfix 54 mm Guardsman figure can now be used as raw material and considerably modified and repositioned to give a man in a specific situation on a appropriate occasion. In actual fact, a diorama depicting the defence of Hougoumont cries out for group treatment — an officer, sergeant, and a

Superb conversion work by Roy Dilley. Above: Trench-raiding party of 1916 interrogate German prisoners. The British are converted from old Britain's metal toy figures, and the Germans are converted plastic motor racing personnel. Below: British infantry, 1915, all converted extensively from old Britain's metal figures with much re-animation. Dioramas are from simple scenic materials, twigs, and home-painted backgrounds.

Top: Inexpensive plastic assembly kits provide a good entry into the model soldier hobby. These well-detailed models are made up from the 1:35 scale Tamiya kit of Red Army infantry of 1943. Middle: Contrasting sources of models in the collection of Chris Ellis. The German drum major in parade dress is a soldat metal custom-painted model while the BMW combination is converted and altered from the standard Britain's item. Bottom: Hinchliffe metal 20 mm Germans, intended for wargaming but also inexpensive collector's pieces for anyone with limited cash or space.

couple of privates defending a portion of the wall — in which case a 'five Ws' exercise would be carried out for each figure in turn to establish his likely character, dress and equipment, and his place in the scene. Even the scenic work for a small diorama can be given a modified form of 'five Ws' consideration for the scenic setting must match the effect conveyed by the figures. A 1916 Western Front trench scene, for instance, is unlikely to be enhanced by a fullflowering tree on the parapet, but a few gaunt branches of blasted tree trunk on the other hand will set the scene and period precisely.

Though the 'five Ws' exercise is described here with the more ambitious type of conversion in mind, it is equally applicable to the simplest of models. You may purchase a cast metal Waffen-SS man in combat dress, a perfectly standard 'collector' quality figure. Your own personal 'five Ws' treatment might determine that he could be the NCO of a machine-gun team on the Russian Front in the hot summer of 1943, so he is simply given a pair of binoculars and his helmet slung from his belt, his original head being changed for a bare head. In the painting stage he would be given a very dusty uniform and a stubbly unshaven chin. Someone else might arrive at an entirely different finish for the same basic figure.

Don't scorn this method of thinking well ahead and establishing and visualising your objectives before you start cutting up figures and playing with paint. Quite apart from the added satisfaction of exercising your imagination in a logical way, there can be other considerations, such as ensuring that you have all the necessary components, parts, and paints before you begin, rather than finding out half way through that a vital part is missing. Allied with this, some pre-planning can make the maximum use of spare parts — for example the head left over from one conversion might be suitable for use on another, and such care can lead to a saving of a fair sum of money in spare parts over a number of years.

8: Plastic Figures

WORKING with any type of plastic figure is generally rather less costly than working in metal, since even the most elaborate plastic kit offerings, such as those made by Historex, are normally less expensive than an equivalent cast metal 'collector' quality piece. In addition, plastic figures are generally quite easy to work with and require only the more basic tools, due to the ease of cutting. There are special points to watch, however, and these we will look at here.

Soft plastics

Cheapest of all model soldiers, these are the 'toy' items which are widely available. The most prolific makers of generally *accurate* 'toy' figures are Air-fix and Britains, but there are others, and it is always worth keeping an eye on toy stockists as new items, some from quite obscure manufacturers, appear from time to time and are worth snapping up. There are plenty of other 'toy' figures around which fall down on anatomical or detail accuracy, or both, but even those ranges which are poor from the scale modeller's point of view have the occasional worthwhile figure which is usable. Airfix offer their famous series of 20/25 mm (sold as 00/HO) figures as well as the 54 mm size. Airfix figures are in polythene, but the most recent Britain's figures are in PVC.

Whichever material is used, however, there are certain limitations inherent in the mass-produced nature of these soft plastic soldiers which must be over-come. Some quite experienced modellers regard this type of figure with horror, but on the other hand cheap plastic figures suitably re-worked have featured in some prize-winning dioramas so effectively that the onlooker would never guess their origin. To make this type of figure cheap, durable, and suitable for quick moulding, the tough, flexible, soft plastic is used by the maker. Examine a batch of these figures and the characteristics become clear; most are one-piece mouldings and the designer adapts the pose (usually most effectively, all things considered) so that it will fit the two halves of the mould and keep undercuts and awkward shapes to a minimum. There is usually a very clear 'parting line' visible all round the figure, at or near the vertical centre-line where the two mould halves join. There may sometimes be some 'flash' (a ridge of superfluous plastic) if the mould is worn and no longer closes up completely. The parting line and any accompanying flash are the big give-aways of the cheap plastic figure. Even in those places which need only painting, it is necessary to eliminate these defects. Allied to the parting lines, various dimples or sink marks are very often visible. With the smaller scale figure, these blemishes are proportionately more obvious.

Hence we come to the first task in working on all soft plastic figures — get-ting rid of the moulding blemishes. With PVC figures, you can use a sharp knife blade and pare off the ridge of the parting line quite safely, plus any flash or other extraneous plastic. If the blade is sharp you should find no great trouble, though care must be taken not to cut too deeply. Generally,

PVC can be cut quite happily and will come off in flake-like pieces; hence quite a lot of conversion work can be done by careful carving, so pockets, shoulder straps, and the like can be removed. Polythene is more difficult to cut, however. It tends to leave a fibrous rough edge if cut with a less than perfect blade, and when cutting off mould lines from a polythene figure it is absolutely essential to use a new sharp pointed blade, your one essential expense. Use a new blade for every session, but you can economise by working on about six soldiers at once as far as this job goes, even if you don't plan to convert or paint all the models in one particular project. Use clean cuts at all times. Filing and sanding must be avoided completely, since this just results in a rough fibrous surface. Very deep undercuts are usually avoided by the maker, and this often leads to a 'web' of plastic left between the forearm and shoulder of a figure firing from the shoulder or carrying a rifle at the high port; look for any such 'web' and cut it away, again with a precise clean cut. Your most used blade for all this work will be a pointed straight-edge type.

Removing flash or parting lines with a knife is more difficult with the small 20/25 mm Airfix figures; one alternative technique which has been used by some is to hold the figure in tweezers and pass it quickly through a candle flame a number of times until the flash and parting line is 'melted' away. This is the most effective method — we've done it for years — though you must be prepared for the occasional disaster, including melting of surface detail and melted limbs. As the figures are cheap and plentiful, however, a few ruined items are hardly noticed. It is important not to leave the figure in the flame — it must be kept moving.

Turning to the figure itself, the designer frequently makes small changes to ease the moulding problems, a common ploy being to switch pieces of equipment around so that they settle conveniently against a substantial part of the figure; the classic example is seen in items like bayonet scabbards, entrenching tools, water-bottle, and other parts hanging from waist level. When the bayonet scabbard hangs from the left side it would normally be suspended clear of the body when kneeling, but polythene or PVC moulding does not lend itself to the delicate undercutting required for this. So the designer will often place the scabbard on the right side of a kneeling figure so that it is moulded against the thigh. Now there can be justification for this in moderation, since the soldiers themselves might take liberties with the arranging of their equipment; generally, however, it is desirable for the serious modeller to correct these deficiencies and put the items in the right places. Sometimes the moulded part can be carefully cut off, trimmed, and used again, but spare parts of pieces made from scrap may have to be substituted. The new pieces need not be of polythene or PVC. They can equally well be hard plastic parts or metal castings. Side arms are another problem. The thin cross-section of a musket, rifle, or sword almost invariably leads to noticeable warping, due to the flexibility of the plastic. Where the side arm is not supported for the greater part of its length, it is usual to replace it if this can be done without too much complication. Where a side arm is held close to the body, however, as in the Airfix marching Highlander, replacing it would be difficult, but on the other hand warping is not so likely to arise in

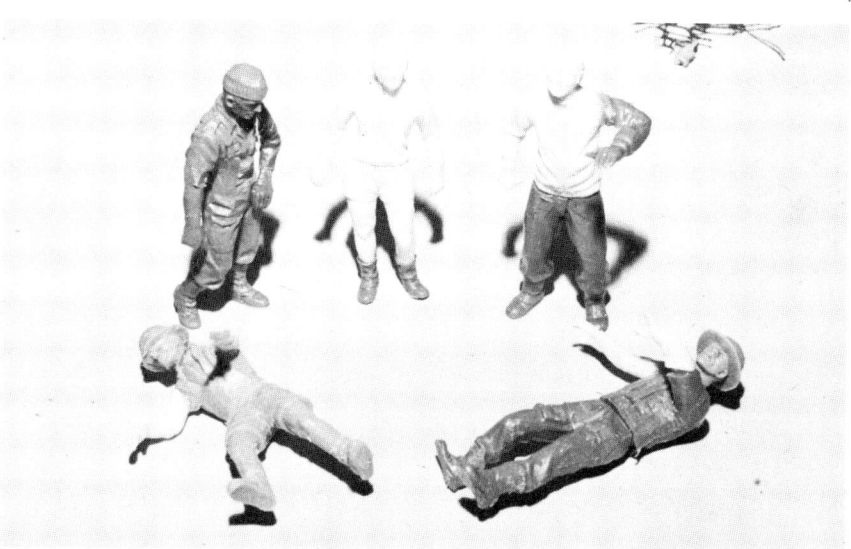

Typical conversion work with cheap Airfix polythene type figures in 54 mm scale, all by John Sandars to make a group of 8th Army soldiers. Top: Lower row shows original figures from various sets as purchased; above them are identical figures cut and re-arranged to give new poses. Above: The five figures resulting from this work, cemented and ready for detailing.

Plastic figures of British infantry, 1815, from the Helmet range. Assembly is simpler than with most other plastic kits, and optional parts are included such as two patterns of shako in this particular kit.

this case.

The absence of deep undercutting can adversely affect the appearance of the equipment. In the Highlander mentioned, the back pack appears to be an extension of the body, with no visible demarcation. In this sort of case the pack must be cut off completely and cemented back in position, replaced with a new piece, or alternatively the sides must be cut away to give a true relief effect. On this same pack, the rolled up greatcoat is no more than a 'bump' on top of the pack, and the task here is to cut it away and replace it with a suitable roll, complete with straps, cut from paper. Summing up the matter, even where no conversion work is contemplated, it is necessary for added realism to give each figure close scrutiny and improve detail appearance wherever this can be safely done.

Actual conversion work, whereby figures in soft plastics are considerably changed, is perfectly feasible, though the wise modeller looks for a suitable pose and changes the details rather than attempts fundamental re-animation. This is because the soft plastics are springy and unyielding, and difficult to glue. Heads can be changed easily enough, since there is a nice working surface, but it is essential to ensure a perfectly flat join. It is possible, also, to drill out a socket inside the collar band of a figure so that a cast metal or hard plastic head may be implanted and cemented. Fairly simple changes like replacing one arm with another are also feasible if the arm in question extends from the body (as with a man throwing a grenade) and is not moulded close up to the trunk. Bent arms may be straightened by cutting a V-shaped gap and working the new shape with the fingers. Five-minute Epoxy, filling the gap, possibly with a small wedge of plastic cemented within the cut, will set the arm in the new position, but it is normally necessary to hold the arm in the new position until the glue sets since the natural springiness of the

Soft Plastics

Pins

Head and arm changing. Drive pins through from outside and snip off flush.

Cut off flash and mould lines with sharp blade

Cut away web of plastic from between arm and weapon.

Top of one figure pinned to bottom of another.

Cut away to separate pack from body.

Replace poorly moulded parts.

Add extra equipment.

Cut away moulded bayonet - replace with new scabbard.

Straightening limbs

Cut out wedge of plastic

5 minute epoxy

carve in folds

reinforce with pin pushed in and nipped off flush

use 5-minute epoxy as filler

Drill out inside collar to take metal head.

Cut

Plastic wedge

Remove original folds. Cement in wedge with 5-minute epoxy.

plastic will tend to make it return to its original position; the small plastic wedge mentioned above helps prevent this. Five-Minute Epoxy is a good filler, incidentally, for soft plastic figures and can be used for small filling jobs, such as eliminating the vent in the back of a jacket when converting the appearance to that of a smock.

Before the advent of the Five-Minute Epoxy, the most effective way of joining items like heads and limbs was by 'universal' cement in conjunction with short lengths of the smallest size of household pins which were used like pegs. The pin was formed into the plastic with pliers, using a larger pin to pierce out a pilot hole. This can still be done, of course, but Five-Minute Epoxy is very effective in holding polythene or PVC and is also excellent for cementing hard plastic or cast metal parts to the soft plastic. Pins can still be used as pegs if desired, but this is not strictly necessary unless a piece is to receive extensive handling or forms an otherwise unsupported part of a diorama group. An example might be a charging figure on one leg, where a pin up through the base of the diorama would secure the piece through the foot. If 'universal' cement is used, it is usual to use pins to secure a figure to the base if the original moulded base is not used. For Britain's Deetail figures, and other PVC types, PVC cement (eg, Britfix 20) can be used, but Five-Minute Epoxy is equally suitable.

The last point about soft plastic figures concerns the preparation for painting. The original method advocated (and still encountered today if you read books and magazines published some years ago) was to scrub each piece in hot soapy water to eliminate the greasy surface and so make ordinary plastic enamels adhere well. In practice this process was limited in its effect, for ordinary modelling paints still wore off, or flaked off the figure, however carefully applied. Also, of course, it is hardly possible to scrub models which have been subjected to conversion or detail work. The modern method which has proved entirely effective is to paint the entire figure thoroughly with Unibond PVA adhesive. While sold as a glue, and milky in appearance, this sets as a hard transparent skin and the figure can then be painted with any type of model paint just like a hard plastic or metal piece. One variation from this rule; PVC figures of the type sold ready-painted by Britain's are in a special PVC paint — in practice we have found that model paints take well straight on this painted surface so long as the original PVC paint surface has not been removed in extensive conversion work. Bear in mind, however, that large areas of some of these figures may not be painted at all — a 'redcoat' figure is likely to be moulded in red PVC with the tunic left unpainted and only the other areas of the figure actually paint covered.

Hard plastics

Nearly all plastic figures sold in kit form are moulded in polystyrene just like virtually all other plastic kits. There are also some complete figures to be found, moulded in hard plastics rather than soft plastics. Among these are the 20/25 mm size pieces in some Airfix and Japanese tank kits; and the Minitanks figures. Some 54 mm or 40 mm figures are ready-moulded in polystyrene too. The serious modeller prefers these hard plastics, mainly because they are the easiest of all materials to work and convert. They join

HORSES

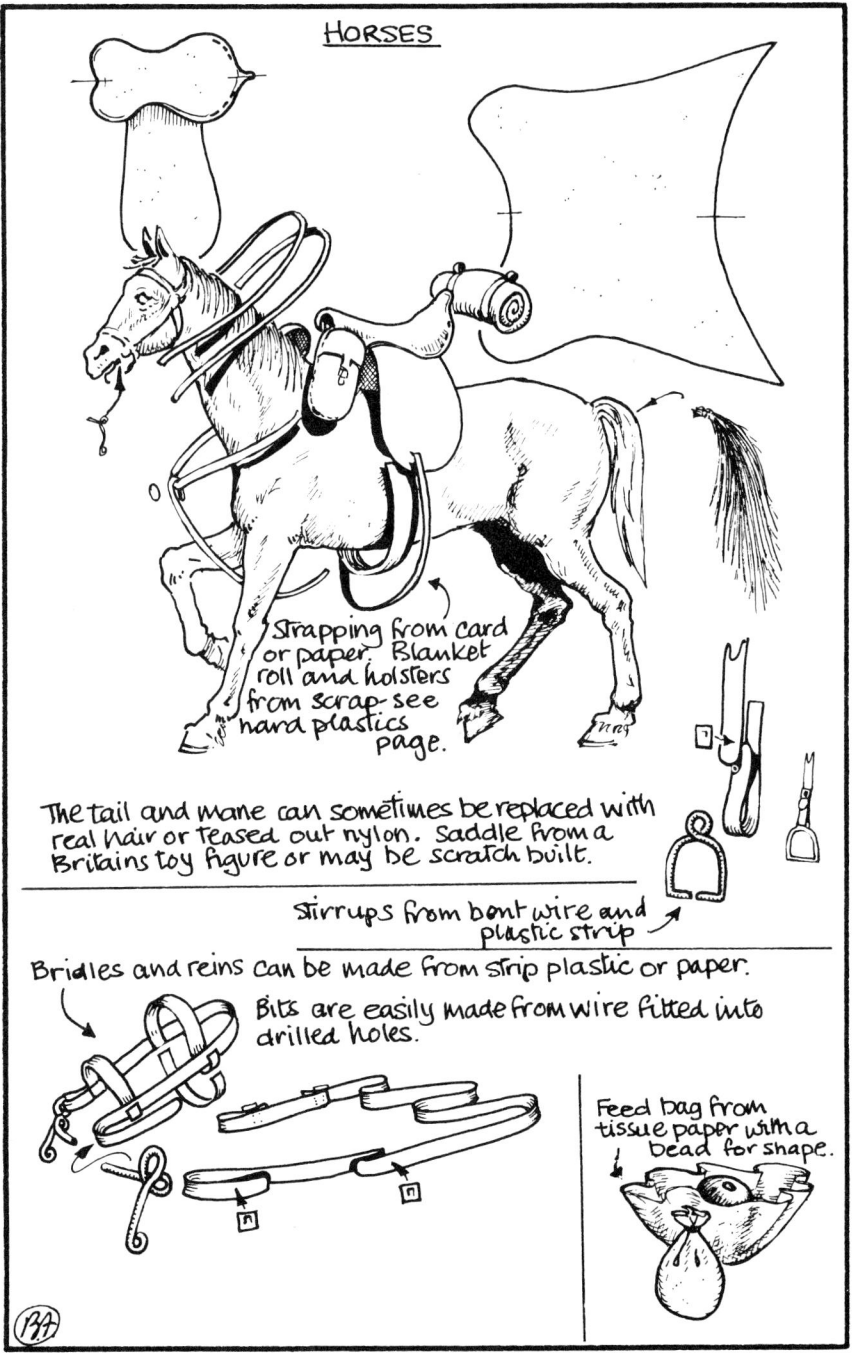

Strapping from card or paper. Blanket roll and holsters from scrap-see hard plastics page.

The tail and mane can sometimes be replaced with real hair or teased out nylon. Saddle from a Britains toy figure or may be scratch built.

Stirrups from bent wire and plastic strip

Bridles and reins can be made from strip plastic or paper.

Bits are easily made from wire fitted into drilled holes.

Feed bag from tissue paper with a bead for shape.

with ordinary polystyrene cements of both the tube and liquid variety, and can be filled with the various proprietory modelling putties on the market. There is almost no limit to the possibilities, and because of the ease of cutting, filing, filling, and cementing, the most extensive conversion work can be carried out. Kits of parts, though intended for a specific figure, can be used as genuine raw material for building a figure of an entirely different period. For instance Ray Anderson has built a whole series of superb models in 54 mm covering the Indian Wars period (both Indians and soldiers) and a fine collection of Samurai warriors using Historex kits as the basis for his work; all the Historex kits concerned are intended for the French First Empire period, but Ray Anderson uses the kits as a source of legs, arms, bodies, heads, and so on, building up the uniform detail and animating as required by altering the parts to suit.

The best way to get acquainted with the possibilities is to purchase one of the cheaper kits in this category, such as one of the Airfix 54 mm offerings, or one of the Tamiya 1:35 scale kits covering groups of World War 2 figures. All the kits give assembly diagrams, but in most cases the assembly sequence is self-evident because the parts generally fit with great precision. Optional parts are frequently given, and a 'dry run' without cement will show where a basic figure can be given a little variation in such matters as leg, arm, and equipment position. Some recent Airfix kits are 'universal', and legs, arms, and bodies may be interchanged without alteration. These hard plastic figures are the easiest of all to re-animate since joints can be cut or sawn through almost at will, and the parts re-cemented in new positions. Care must be taken to modify the fit of the clothing consequent to any changes (as explained in the previous chapter), and it is a fairly easy matter to fill gaps or build up any areas with plastic putty. The components of these plastic kits are usually extremely delicate, and the utmost care must be taken in cutting them from the sprue or runner. The usual rule is to leave parts on the sprue until needed, to obviate the risk of loss. Larger components can be assembled with tube glue, but with some of the very tiny parts like the buttons and separate 'acorns' supplied in Historex kits, liquid cement is a necessity. The part can be held either with a pin or tweezers in its precise position, then secured by just a drop of liquid cement applied by brush point.

After main assembly is complete, any slight 'ooze' of cement between adjacent parts can be rubbed down when set, using a fine file, glass paper, or emery board. Make good any defects or sink marks with plastic puttty. Some modellers prefer to keep fine detail, such as orders and decorations, until the entire model is finished and painted. The small parts concerned (eg, the 'star' of an order) is then painted on the sprue, cut-away when dry, touched up, and cemented to the already-painted figure with a touch of Five-Minute Epoxy or ACC — polystyrene cement will not work on a painted surface. Surface detail and texture on polystyrene models is invariably finely moulded and very delicate. It can be damaged easily by careless knife or file work, and any spillage of cement can be harmful. If the worst happens and a blob of cement is dropped by accident, do not attempt to remove it while still wet; this will simply smear the cement over an even larger area of plastic — wait until the blob is dry, then remove it with a knife, file, or by sanding.

Hard Plastics

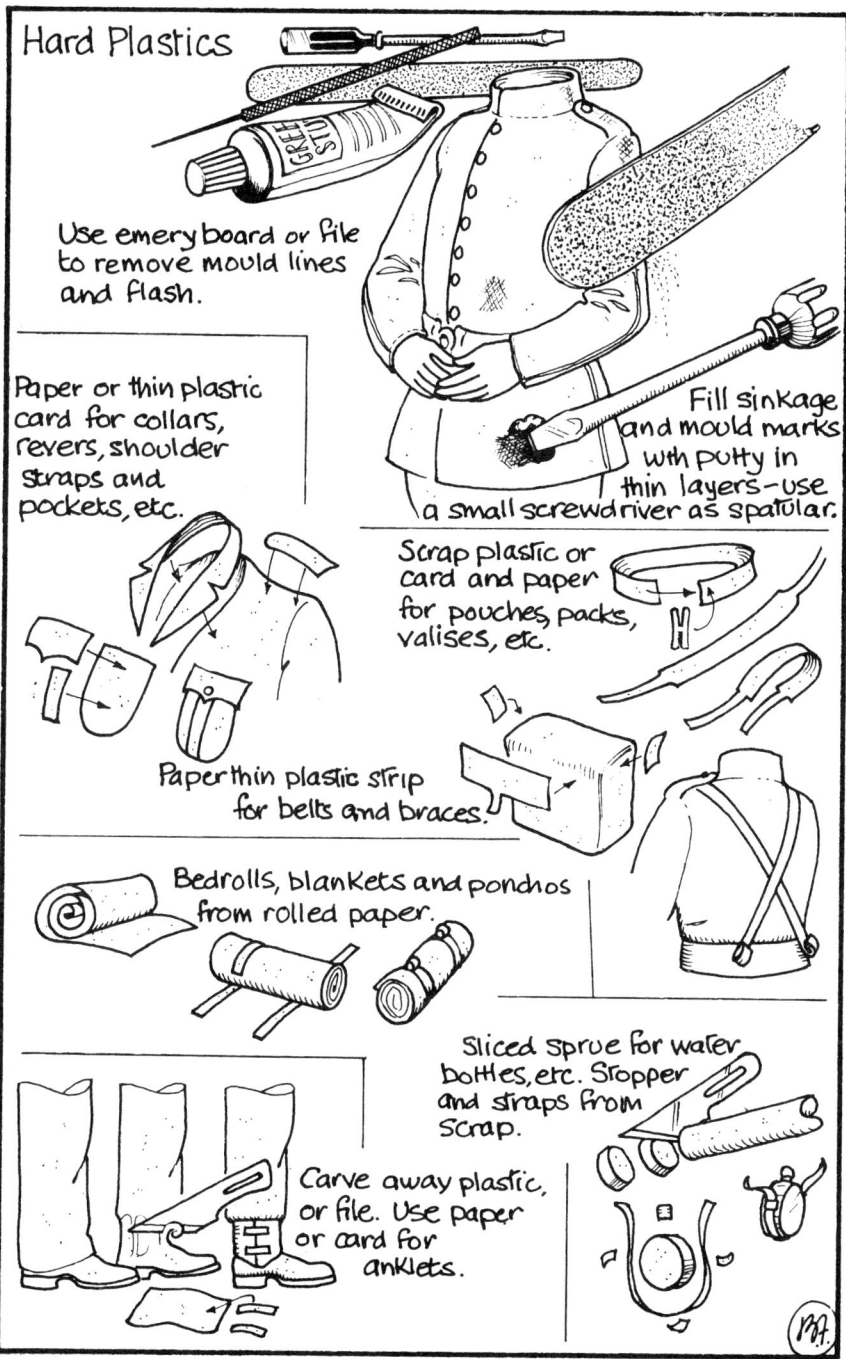

Use emery board or file to remove mould lines and flash.

Paper or thin plastic card for collars, revers, shoulder straps and pockets, etc.

Fill sinkage and mould marks with putty in thin layers—use a small screwdriver as spatular.

Scrap plastic or card and paper for pouches, packs, valises, etc.

Paper thin plastic strip for belts and braces.

Bedrolls, blankets and ponchos from rolled paper.

Sliced sprue for water bottles, etc. Stopper and straps from scrap.

Carve away plastic, or file. Use paper or card for anklets.

file off original folds

Saw or cut half-way through

Bend gently

fill in with Greenstuff

file or etch in new creases and folds

Saw off unwanted limb or part- clean up area.

Cut off pouch

fill in belt detail

Putty here

file here

Cement new limb into place - make good area with body putty and file.

'Spare part' limbs can be filed and butted to any angle

Pyrogravure or hot needle to shape hair or mouth.

Remove head

file neck fill in gap

Cement in new position make collar from paper

hollow out cheeks

B.F.

Extensive use can be made of plastic card and plastic strip when detailing hard plastic figures. Indeed a plain figure completely devoid of detail can be given a full outfit of equipment, plus such features as tunic lapels and shoulder straps, all built up from thin plastic card or paper. Modelling ribbon of the type included in Historex and Airfix kits is specially suitable, of course, for fine strapping, but parcel tape or gift wrapping tape can be used in the same way, cutting fine slivers of material as required.

Cast metal parts can be mixed at will with plastic parts if Five-Minute Epoxy is used as the adhesive. The Pyrogravure, mentioned in Chapter 4, is a very handy tool for the prolific modeller working with plastic figures. It allows considerable re-modelling of moulded parts to give them an entirely different appearance. For instance the nostrils of a horse can be 'flared', his ears set back, his mane set 'flying' all by working over the plastic surface with the needle of the machine. A man's cheeks may be 'hollowed', his mouth re-shaped from closed to open, new folds and tucks etched into a tunic and so on ad infinitum. While the Pyrogravure is in no way a necessary purchase it certainly opens up very considerable possibilities for the ambitious modeller. Very similar effects can be obtained, incidentally, by the use of a heated needle held in pliers, though the degree of control is poor and it is not commended for youngsters or beginners. However, for the odd job, such as altering the shape of a mouth, a red-hot needle is worth using, but with great care!

When it comes to horses, there is a great degree of flexibility. Historex produce the bodies, heads, limbs, etc, of their horses in such a way that almost all components match up throughout the range. Thus from a dozen or so assorted halves it is possible to arrive at over 80 different assemblies, giving huge variety in finished appearance. As all the parts can be purchased separately, there is no real need to duplicate horse positions in a given group. The horses in the Airfix range do not offer such flexibility, but even so parts can be interchanged between kits to give some variety, and some modellers combine Airfix and Historex parts — which is perfectly feasible — to give yet further variation. The Britain's horses, though PVC and ready-moulded also come in a number of different forms and it is, of course, possible to mount a polystyrene figure on a suitably detailed Britain's horse. Indeed, for the impecunious modeller, there are several fine horses in the Britain's range at ridiculously low prices. Saddles and harness, if required for conversion work, can be made up from paper, plastic strip, and other materials, exactly as for soldiers' personal equipment.

Of all the hard plastic figures, those made in kit form by Historex are generally regarded as the finest and they set the standard by which all others are judged. The newcomer to the hobby should certainly invest in the Historex catalogue, for in addition to illustrating the vast extent of the range the catalogue is in itself a valuable reference aid as it gives a grounding in the soldiers of the Napoleonic period, is beautifully illustrated, and includes many tips and articles on assembly and painting of hard plastic figures. You may not actually be interested in the Napoleonic period as such, but the pieces can form the basis of conversions for virtually any period by judicious selection from the parts list.

Two typical assembly variations possible with Historex horse components.

A figure sold as a ready-moulded complete piece in polystyrene can be treated as for a kit so far as conversion and detailing potential is concerned. What will be found almost invariably, however, is a parting line, possibly some flash, and the usual sink or die marks. These need to be eliminated, just as they do with soft plastic figures, but in the case of hard polystyrene figures a file or emery board can be used for the task.

It only remains to say that once assembly and conversion work is completed on a hard plastic figure, it can in theory be painted directly over the plastic. It is advisable, though, to give a flat primer undercoat — matt white or grey is commended — since any imperfections in the work, such as poor joins, excess cement, or 'strings' of adhesive, will show up through the primer and can then be remedied. It may be too late to do this conveniently if, say, a 'string' of cement only becomes visible when the neat scarlet of a tunic has been carefully painted in.

76

9: Metal Figures

AS we have seen, while metal or 'tin' soldiers formed the basis of the 'toy' market for many decades, the metal soldiers generally available today are the 'collector' type figure, cast in solid metal which may be pewter or near-pewter or a cruder alloy made of varying proportions of lead/antimony and tin. This substance is fairly soft, thus allowing a degree of bending which is necessary for animation in some types of figure.

The metal figure today does, in fact, come in several forms. Very popular, and much produced is the ready-assembled, animated casting, which is often what might be called a 'portrait pose', usually a simple standing position. This type of figure starts as a spread-eagled casting and the maker's animator assembles the piece for sale. The legs are positioned and soldered or glued to a base (which may itself by either sheet metal or cast), and the arms are bent to some suitable pose. The same basic figure may be produced in several slightly differing poses — a rifleman with weapon at the order, at the shoulder, at the slope, or slung, for example, each of these variations offering the purchaser a degree of individuality. The side-arms, pack, and other accessories are often separate castings put on by the maker at assembly stage. This type of ready-assembled figure is frequently available ready-painted to special order, though normally only unpainted castings (at best merely primered) are offered for sale. Some makers actually cast their figures fully animated, most Series 77 pieces being so produced, for example; in other words this type of figure will be cast with its limbs in a set position rather as soft plastic figures are turned out.

The other major type of metal figure is sold in kit form. These kits are not so elaborate as the plastic kits, and a typical kit might consist of a complete body and legs, two separate arms, pack and equipment, and side-arms, plus a base. Some small degree of variation is possible in the way the kit is assembled. A cast arm may be bent at the elbow, or the actual angle of the arm can be adjusted. Thus a figure which the maker intends to be assembled carrying his musket at the high port might possibly be assembled in the shoulder firing position, with head and arm angles altered accordingly. Conversion possibilities are quite extensive, though the work involved is not, perhaps, as easy as in a hard plastic figure. However, the same sort of detailing, adding and altering of equipment, etc, is perfectly feasible. Hard or soft plastic parts can be incorporated if Five-Minute Epoxy is used as an adhesive. Many cast figures show a parting line just as the plastic ones do, and this must be carefully filed down and removed before painting. Even figures sold fully assembled and ready to paint should be checked over in this respect.

Firms such as Rose, Lasset, and H-R, sell many cast metal components separately, all valuable pieces for use in conversions, either with plastic or metal figures. Of special note are the heads in distinctive types of headgear, sold by Rose and essential for much conversion work.

Generally speaking — though there are some exceptions — cast metal figures are more expensive, piece for piece, than even the most expensive plastic kits. For this reason, those who purchase cast metal figures are usually less inclined to risk their investment in a complicated conversion. Opinions vary over the respective merits of plastic and cast metal figures, some collectors scorning plastics and avoiding them completely. There is no doubt that the weight and feel of a metal 'collector' figure is one of its big attractions— the piece is substantial and stands rigid, whereas plastic figures are feather light, however beautifully detailed they might be. The model soldier hobby, however, offers something for everyone. Those who lack the time, skill, or inclination for actual kit assembly or extensive re-working of basic figures can buy ready-made metal pieces, while those who wish to be creative can spend many happy hours working with plastic parts. It is a free choice which you alone can make.

The final category of metal figure is the vintage 'toy', notably from Britains. It is possible to start collecting second-hand figures of this type in near 'mint' condition provided you have the money to pay the high prices asked. There are several specialist dealers who advertise in the hobby magazines. These dealers also sell battered imperfect examples at rather lower prices. Club meetings and exhibitions often have one or more specialist dealer in attendance with stock on sale. The collector specialising in vintage figures usually displays (or keeps) his models in their original 'toy' condition. If you have a source of reference, such as a catalogue, it is easy enough to restore battered but complete models to the original appearance by stripping off the paint (using ordinary proprietory paint stripper), priming the casting, and painting it up to resemble the original style — using glossy paint if you are a purist on the matter.

Very battered and broken or incomplete Britain's figures can be acquired for much lower prices. These may lack heads, arms, bases, and possibly be holed. While the castings are stripped of paint, as before, restoration involves replacing any missing pieces (Rose heads are useful here) and blocking any holes with plastic putty, Plastic Padding, or a similar filler. B.S. Armstrong fills such restored pieces with lead shot in polyurethane varnish to give them 'heft', drilling a suitable hole in an inconspicuous part of the casting. This makes the model virtually solid and prevents further deterioration. Having dealt with physical restoration, painting can take place. Here one has the choice of choosing an original Britain's regiment, or doing what several collectors do and painting the models as types and regiments that the Britain's firm never got round to. Some modellers who acquire old broken Britain's models are not concerned with restoration, and simply use them as in the old days as the basis for conversion work. This is a matter of personal choice.

Flats, though metal figures, are a law unto themselves. Few collectors convert them, for the makers turn out variety enough. Flats, in short, are mainly collected for their own special appeal, and most of the effort goes into painting or diorama work.

Whatever sort of metal figure interests you, its surface must be suitably prepared before painting. Some ready-made 'collector' pieces are sold fully primered and in all respects ready to paint. Others come in bare metal, and a model made or converted in metal is, of course, in the same state. The modern technique is to paint the entire model very thoroughly with

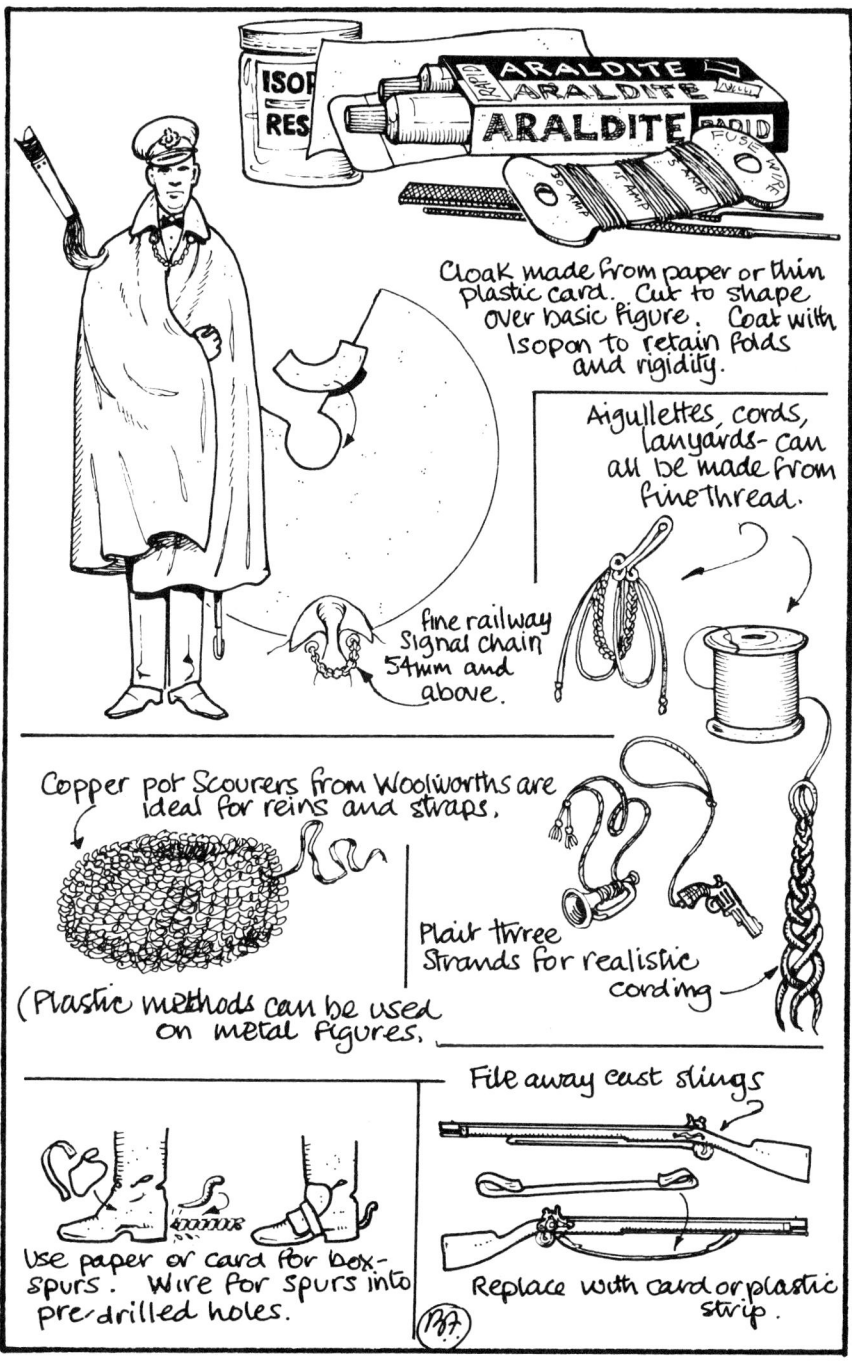

Cloak made from paper or thin plastic card. Cut to shape over basic figure. Coat with Isopon to retain folds and rigidity.

Aigullettes, cords, lanyards- can all be made from fine thread.

fine railway signal chain 54mm and above.

Copper pot Scourers from Woolworths are ideal for reins and straps.

Plait three strands for realistic cording

(Plastic methods can be used on metal figures.

Use paper or card for box-spurs. Wire for spurs into pre-drilled holes.

File away cast slings

Replace with card or plastic strip.

79

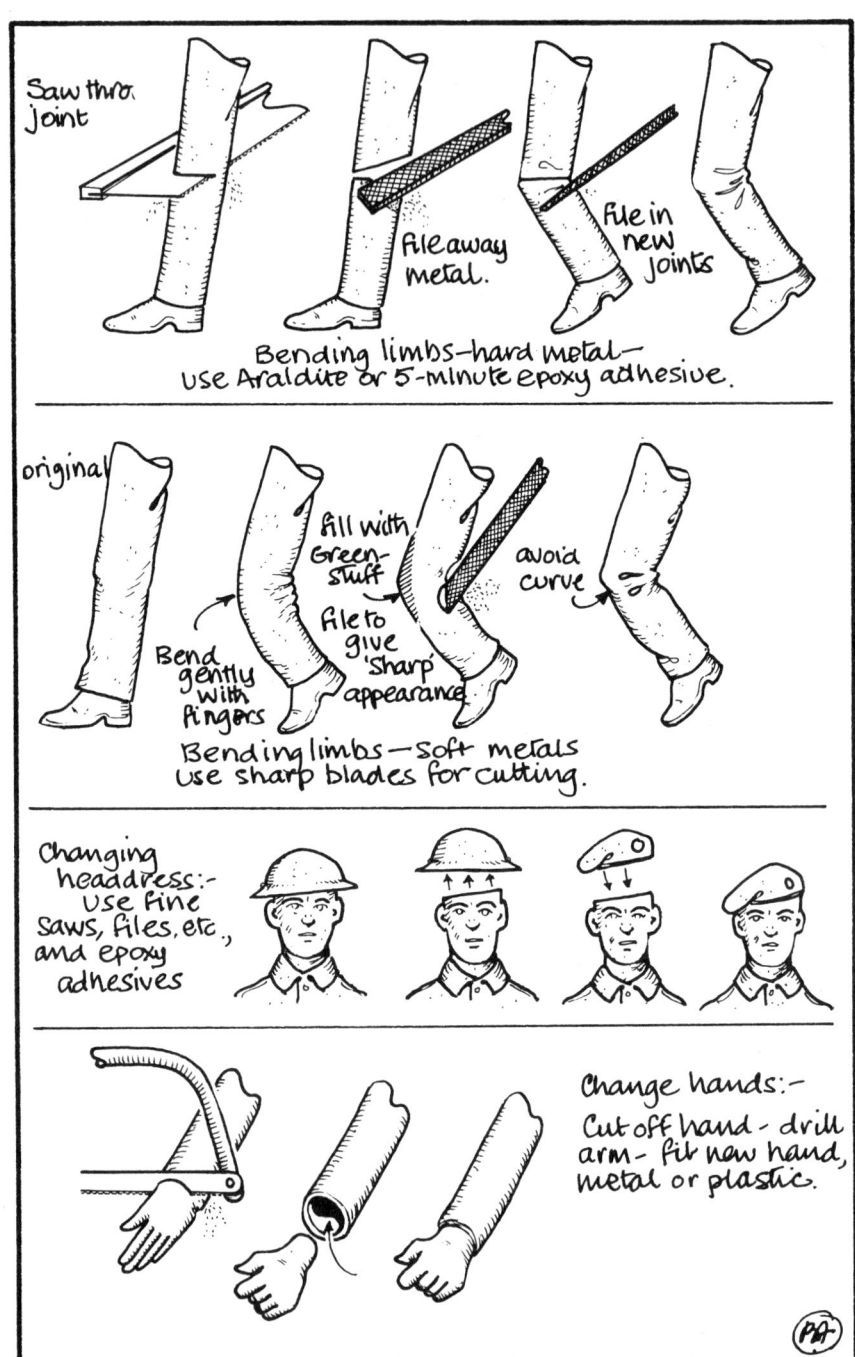

Saw thro' joint

File away metal.

File in new joints

Bending limbs—hard metal—
use Araldite or 5-minute epoxy adhesive.

original

Bend gently with fingers

Fill with Green-stuff

File to give 'sharp' appearance

avoid curve

Bending limbs—soft metals
use sharp blades for cutting.

Changing headdress:-
use fine saws, files, etc.,
and epoxy adhesives

Change hands:-
Cut off hand - drill
arm - fit new hand,
metal or plastic.

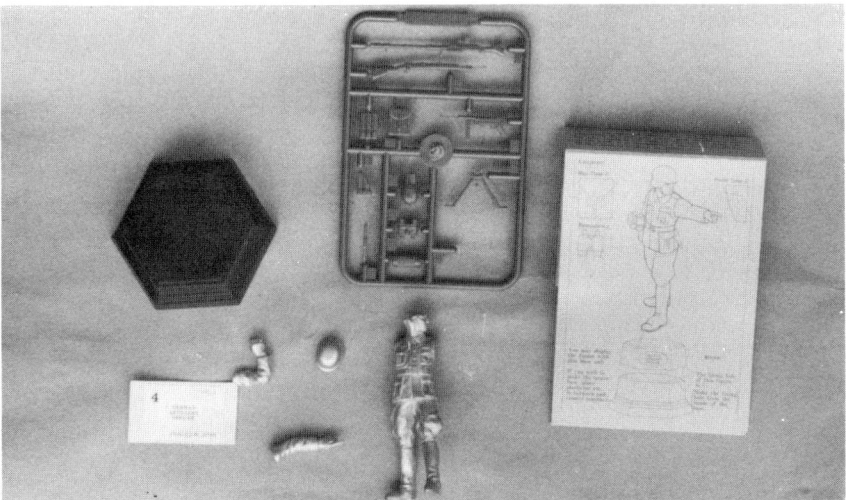

Top: Fine conversions of old Britain's metal figures, by John Ruddle, to make the 1815 period Corps of Drums of the 57th Foot. Drums are made from scratch as described in this book. Above: Typical metal kit, in this case 75 mm (1:25 scale) by Tamiya, with plastic plinth and accessories.

polyurethane varnish (matt) working the varnish well into every recess. This gives an air-tight covering and should help preserve the model for all time from that old bogey 'lead disease' which is caused by the oxidisation of the lead content. Many an old model has been ruined this way, the oxidisation even attacking a complete painted model. A matt primer coat of plastic enamel is commended over the polyurethane covering to form a good basis for the final coat of paint. As with plastic figures, this will also show up any imperfections in the assembly or details of the model before it is too late.

It is possible to assemble cast metal figure kits with low melting point solder (which is liquid at 80-100 degrees C), but don't be tempted to do this if you are not already familiar with the use of a soldering iron. A clumsy move can ruin an expensive model. Cast figures can be assembled perfectly well with adhesive.

While most of the foregoing remarks are applicable to models of 54 mm size and larger, it should be observed that, with a few exceptions, metal figures in all the smaller scales come as one-piece castings complete with base. All the procedures described are equally applicable to these smaller pieces, and particular attention should be paid to eliminating mould marks.

10: Painting

HOWEVER well you make or convert a model, its final appearance will stand or fall by its painting. The finest model can look utterly unconvincing if poorly painted, while a run of the mill piece can be made into a winner with a top class finish. When it comes to painting, moreover, a good many modellers take fright and either end up with a lot of unpainted figures, or else make a hash of early attempts and opt out of the hobby disappointed at their failings.

Rather than be discouraged, however, the novice modeller should approach the subject methodically. A basic painting kit might comprise the following:

(1) Paint brushes in sizes 0, 00, 1, 2, 3 and at least one small chisel-edged brush. Plus at least one old but serviceable brush for base coat work with Unibond or polyurethane varnish.

(2) Thinners and brush cleaner as sold by the model paint makers.

(3) Some small mixing palettes, which could be made from foil pie dishes, plastic container lids, old jar tops, or any similar shallow receptacles.

(4) Tissues and/or a cloth.

The old advice about using good quality brushes always holds good. The major art supply manufacturers make excellent sable or squirrel hair brushes which are not cheap, but last for years if kept scrupulously clean and well looked after. Cheap 'toyshop' paint brushes which quickly shed their bristles are a false economy. Keep your basic painting gear in a good box, if possible with a separate compartment (or an old pencil box) for the brushes, to ensure they are not crushed or damaged while stored.

There is now an enormous range of suitable paints. Firms like Humbrol and Testor make extensive ranges of model paints which are sold in tinlets or small bottles and are a familiar sight in hobby stores and toyshops. For the average modeller these paints will fulfill all requirements, but the model figure hobby has come up with many paints which have been formulated specially for model soldiers. Campaign, Plaka, Rose, and Historex all produce paints of good quality which can be commended. These ranges are particularly good for ceremonial type dress, the scarlets, blues, and greens giving both realistic colouring and lifelike texture. Some advanced modellers use gouache and polymer paints, and others use oil paints; there is nothing to stop any novice experimenting in this direction, but the price can be high. Other paints available are Polly S, which is water soluble and thus very easy to use, and Floquil which is of excellent quality. Floquil make a special 'barrier' coat for their paint which should be applied to any plastic surface before the paint is used, as this particular formulation attacks some plastic surfaces.

While restored 'toy' figures may require gloss paints, as used on the old Britain's models, virtually all other model soldiers are painted in matt, since uniforms and flesh are matt in real life. The exceptions to this general rule are leather items like boots and belts and leggings, and brass or metal parts and varnished wood equipment. Even these are rarely as glossy model paint, and

Top: The figures shown on page 67 are here pictured on completion. Heads and faces are painted and the bodies are in basic colours. Figures are pinned temporarily to wood block bases for ease of handling. Note figures at each end with added outer garments from adhesive tape and paper respectively. Above: The same figures fully painted — note the dry-brushing to give dusty 'desert sand' effect. Poses are chosen for a specific diorama project.

gloss clear varnish applied over matt paint is usually sufficient. It is a good idea for a beginner to acquire the leaflets and lists put out by the major model paint makers since these often include colour patches. Anyone starting new to the hobby could play safe and buy one of the 'uniform' paint sets sold by Humbrol, or the constituent paints which Humbrol list for this set.

A basic set of paints could comprise the following:

(1) Gloss clear varnish, matt clear varnish, black, white, mid-grey (shade not crucial), yellow, 'flesh', 'wood', leather', 'gun metal' 'silver', 'brass', dark brown (all these matt).

(2) Add to these the colours suitable for the figures you are modelling, eg, field grey and dark grey, red, pink, etc, for Germans of World War 2, or all 'full dress' colours for the Napoleonic period.

Keep all colours in a box for safety and long life. Paint can be expensive these days, so keep all tins and bottles sealed. Check the quality from time to time and stir the paints that are used less frequently to stop the pigment solidifying out in the bottom of the pot. Replace any paints if a skin forms or the paint becomes lumpy. All oil-based model paints must be stirred very thoroughly before use.

Before starting to paint a figure check that you have a block of wood or some other suitable scrap to which it may be clipped or pegged by its base, thus giving you a 'handle' and reducing the need for touching the figure itself. In the early stages of painting you may well be able to grasp the actual figure, but touching recently painted areas as work proceeds may damage the paint-work. Clothes pegs, bulldog clips, or drawing pins (depending on the base) can be used to attach the figure to the wood. The other important point is to make a last check out of the figure to ensure that it actually is finished! Many modellers have lovingly painted up figures only to have a critical admirer point out later than the water bottle or some such item is missing; with many small details to remember in a complicated conversion it is only too easy to overlook something.

There are many ways of painting a figure, and you may well evolve your own techniques. However, for those with no particular preference the most usual order is (1) face and other flesh areas; (2) tunic; (3) trousers; (4) head gear; (5) equipment, side-arms, etc; (6) boots and leggings; (7) buttons, buckles, small metal parts (eg, badges); (8) fine piping and other distinctions not previously covered; (9) lining out and picking out of any detail, artificial shading, etc; (10) stand or base if applicable (single figures).

This sequence ensures that what most modellers find most difficult — the facial area — is done first. The sequence applies particularly to figures of 54 mm size and larger where detail painting is feasible. If you work in the smaller scales you may wish to simplify this a lot. For example 20/25 mm size faces can be depicted by little more than the flesh colouring since the figure is so tiny, and only those with a very steady hand would be able to paint in badges and piping in this scale, let alone such details as kilt tartans.

If you examine any figures painted by the experts you'll note that dynamic realism is achieved by the very skilful use of shading and highlighting, both on the uniform and on the flesh areas. This is exactly analogous to techniques used in stage, film, or TV make-up where over-emphasis (eye-shading,

Top: Close view of painted face detail by Arthur Woolford (shown much larger than actual size). Above: Three female warriors made by Arthur Woolford (from left: Ancient Briton, Phrygian, and Greek Amazon) showing painting of subtle detail such as woad.

highlighting, etc) is employed to compensate for strong lighting (which reduces natural shadows) and the long viewing distance (in relative terms) of the audience. Shadows will be cast naturally on a model figure, but both daylight and average artificial light is too intense and diffuse relative to the size of a small figure, so we do what a stage director would do and virtually 'make-up' the figure to improve its appearance by accentuating the shadows and highlights.

Flesh, and the face in particular, is the most difficult of parts to paint. Flesh colour paints used straight from the tin are rather pink and baby-like, whereas real flesh comes in a whole range of tones. It is here that it is most important to have a mixing tray, for the lighter and deeper tones, and the

85

highlights and shading must be carefully blended with each other; harsh demarcation would give a false doll-like effect (eg, blobs of pink in the middle of the cheeks might look alright on a toy, but are not a realistic representation). It is impractical to take differing colours from a number of different paint tins and work them in with each other on the model face; so small blobs of the various colours you'll need are put into the tray — flesh, red, yellow, black, brown, white. They can be judiciously mixed as required for each. The entire area of the face and neck is painted with the basic flesh colour, and all the other tones needed are painted on in quick succession while the base coat is still wet. Brown or black is worked in round the chin and cheeks — more for a stubbly face — and the flesh colour is darkened and then painted in to the eye sockets, down the sides of the nose, and from the counters of the nose to the mouth, merging these in all the time so that hard lines of dark colour are avoided. A little red is mixed with the flesh colour for the lips, and more flesh colour and white can be mixed into the paint (on the palette) to lessen the amount of red and provide a highlight area round the cheeks and cheekbones. Inside the ear is shadowed, and false shadow needs darkening in beneath the chin and on the neck. Hands, bare feet, and other bare flesh where applicable gets the same treatment, so that muscle contours, the space between fingers or toes, and so on are shaded and highlighted. Where a sleeve or foot emerges from a sleeve or trouser leg, then false shadow is painted in, using a darker tone and merging it away into the basic flesh tone. If in doubt as to where shading and highlighting should appear, then study close up photographs, or pose your own (or a friend's) face in a mirror at an angle similar to that of the model and observe how the shadows and highlights form in normal daylight viewing.

The whites of the eyes can be painted in after the eye socket as a whole has been shaded and allowed to dry, though you may need to return to it later to line the upper or lower lids (mascara fashion) for better effect. The pupil can be added in very small models (54 mm and below) with the point of a wood cocktail stick, or a pin point. In 54 mm (and 30/40 mm if you have a very steady hand) it is possible to put a highlight into the iris as a tiny spot of white. Ensure that pupils are parallel, and looking in a logical direction in relation to the head position, and the situation of the model. In other words a soldier loading his musket is unlikely to be looking out of the corner of his eyes at the next man! He will be looking down and concentrating on the loading procedure.

Take into account ethnic types, of course. An oriental face will avoid a reddish tone altogether and you would add yellow or ochre to the basic flesh colour. The high cheek bones need empahsising with darker shading (relative to the 'white' man), and there is less shading of the eye socket, the eye itself being usually shallower and the slant, if anything, over-emphasised for effect. With dark-skinned figures, either of the Indian or African type, the flesh colour is not, of course, used as a basic covering. Here a dark brownish shade is used, but it is best to use it rather lighter than you might think accurate; this is because a very dark covering will tend to give a black face 'Mammy' effect completely obliterating the subtleties of the facial features. There tends to be a noticeable gleam on a dark face, and completely matt colours are to be

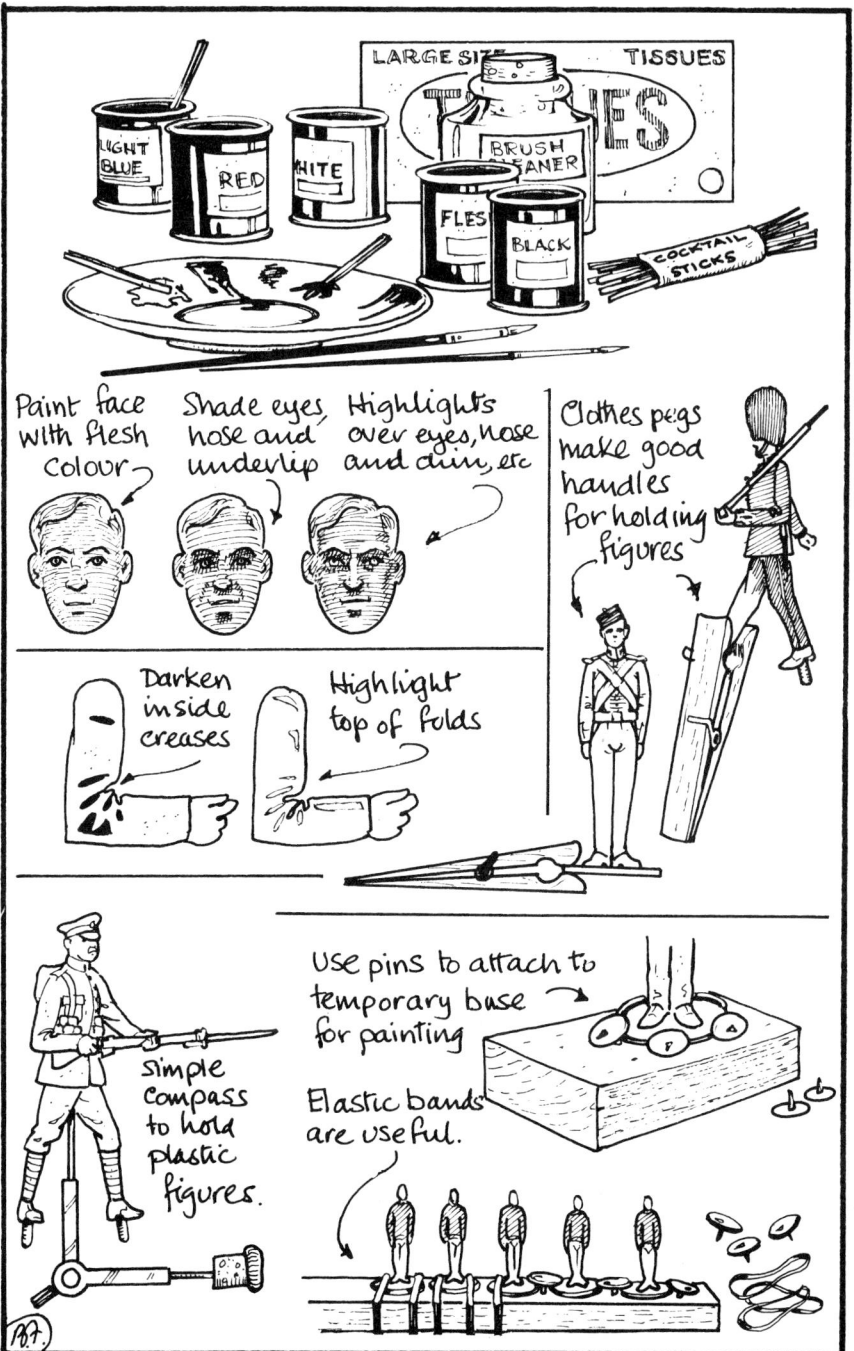

Paint face with flesh colour

Shade eyes nose and underlip

Highlights over eyes, nose and chin, etc

Clothes pegs make good handles for holding figures

Darken inside creases

Highlight top of folds

Simple compass to hold plastic figures.

Use pins to attach to temporary base for painting

Elastic bands are useful.

LARGE SIZE TISSUES

BRUSH CLEANER

LIGHT BLUE

RED

WHITE

FLES

BLACK

COCKTAIL STICKS

Perfection in painting technique; this superb 90 mm Post Militaire Cuirassier of 1811 was made and painted by the designer, Ray Lamb. Note the subtle highlighting and shading, even on the breastplate rivets and belt. This larger view (about twice actual size) acts as a good guide to finished effect for the novice painter to study.

avoided in this case. We have found the Humbrol shade sold as 'Track Colour' to be a good basis for dark faces, though other similar shades could be used. This colour is meant to give the rusty, dirty, effect of old rail track, but it is rather too bright and too 'red' even for this. It has the advantage of being semi-matt (in common with other Humbrol Railway Enamels) which gives a good 'gleam' effect. For Red Indians, this colour needs only slight darkening, but add further black for Indians and even more for Africans. Adding matt black suffices generally to take the 'newness' out of the semi-matt colour but leave enough sheen for the 'gleam' effect. Shading and highlighting is less obvious on a dark face; some modellers don't worry about it at all, but the areas of very dark shadow — eye sockets, eyes, and beneath the chin can be darkened to advantage, even on a 'black' face.

The hair can be painted after the flesh areas are dealt with. The hair may well be oiled in some cases so needs to be semi-matt (varnish can achieve this effect), but it may equally well be entirely matt, as in the case with the 'powdered' styles of the 18th century. The eyebrows are sometimes darker than the head hair. In general, however, painting the hair is a minor point which can be dealt with depending on the type of model.

The main clothing — tunic and lower garments — are in general painted as for the face, with shading and highlighting as appropriate. On clothing it is easier to work out where the shadows and highlights fall because the folds are nearly always moulded into the figure. Thus, when painting a scarlet tunic, take a blob of scarlet on to the palette and work a little black or dark grey into it. Once the tunic is painted the overall scarlet colour, switch straight to the darkened blob of scarlet and start working this into the areas of the folds. It is not really possible to use white as a highlighting toner on strong colours like scarlet and green, for if you do so you will end up with pink or light green. So as a general rule, leave these strong colours to form their own natural highlights on the ridges of folds. A touch of white can be used with good effect in lighter clothing colours like khaki drill, or 'butternut', however, and worked on to the ridges of folds. Darken folds to suit (some folds may throw a stronger shadow than others) and don't forget that areas of shadow may appear under arms and crotch.

The detail painting (stages 5 to 10 in the sequence) will, of course vary considerably with the figure. In general, highly polished leather can be painted in matt colours and varnished to give a gloss afterwards. This will give good natural highlights with no real need to do it artificially. Again, remember that the Humbrol Railway Enamels, being semi-matt, can be used quite extensively, often obviating the need to depict gloss or polish areas with varnish. Some other colours (including Humbrol 'Military Equipment' shades) are also to be had in pleasing semi-matt finish.

Some utilisation can be made of decals, either the waterslide or dryprint types, in detailing and insignia work. Some of the makers of hard plastic models include decal sets in the kits, and one or two have been made by the specialist decal firms over the years. It is mostly German models which have been accorded this luxury, and such items as shoulder strap lacing, iron crosses, medal ribbons, specialist badges, and so on have been produced, all to 54 mm size and most useful if you can get them. The kits concerned usually include spare decal items which can be kept and used on other models. Some dryprint decals (like those made by Blick and Letraset) yield useful items, though not actually intended for model soldiers. Consult the Letraset catalogue, for instance and you'll find 'dots' and chevrons and striping in various colours. Blick do some sheets (including cheap ones for modellers) with similar usable items, though we repeat, that you have to see what's available and what can be utilised for a particular model. As a simple example, however, the finest red stripes made by Blick makes excellent trouser piping, and white stripes can be used for tunic piping, and so on. It is possible to loosen these dryprint items by rubbing them on the backing sheet until they are on the point of coming off, then transferring them to the model. They are only practical though on a simple model — a soldier standing at attention, for instance, for you cannot easily 'bend' the piping round the knee if the figure is kneeling. Some 'dots' can be found occasionally in 'gold' or 'silver' and these make fine buttons if suitable in size. 'Stars' can be used for star-plates on helmets, and such transfers can be modified by careful painting once they are in situ on the model. A decal star-plate may not be quite the right shape but it is an easy enough matter to touch it up slightly with a fine brush once it is applied to the helmet. The use of decals like this depends very much on your own imagination and ingenuity.

Applying decals is a very good example of an instance where a peg or clamp to hold the model firmly, but without damage, is a useful accessory since it leaves both hands free for what can be a fiddling task. With waterslide decals the item can be positioned exactly with the point of a pin or tweezers; with dryprint decals, cut out the area of backing sheet adjacent to the items in use, so that the backing can be held over its position on the model with tweezers while the design is actually transferred. The full sheet of a dryprint decal set is, of course, too unwieldy to handle over the model.

Previous chapters have already stated the need for a primer undercoat before the final finish is applied. In general a matt oil-based model paint is sufficient, white or mid-grey for choice. Some modellers prefer to use a household matt emulsion paint, however, which certainly gives a very smooth finish, and is particularly effective on cast metal models. Metallic areas get a better final finish if a suitable matt undercoat is applied to the area first — white for a 'silver' breastplate, yellow for gold lace or brass. These undercoats give added 'depth' to the metallic finish.

While on the subject of metallic finishes, it is worth remarking that self-adhesive foil coverings, like those sold under the trade names of Metalskin and Baremetal, can be used on larger scale models where body armour is depicted. This material is sold for scale model aircraft, but can be equally effective on, say, a large scale model knight. The various panels are cut to shape to suit the model, and in the case of knights, and the like, the exact size can be achieved for each panel by making paper templates. These are drawn out roughly for each panel or component, tested and trimmed to give an accurate fit, then traced round on the foil covering to give a precise panel shape. Use of templates ensures that full account is taken of the complex curvatures which are encountered in body armour. Rather more messy, but a cheaper alternative, is to use ordinary cooking foil in the same way. This can be af-

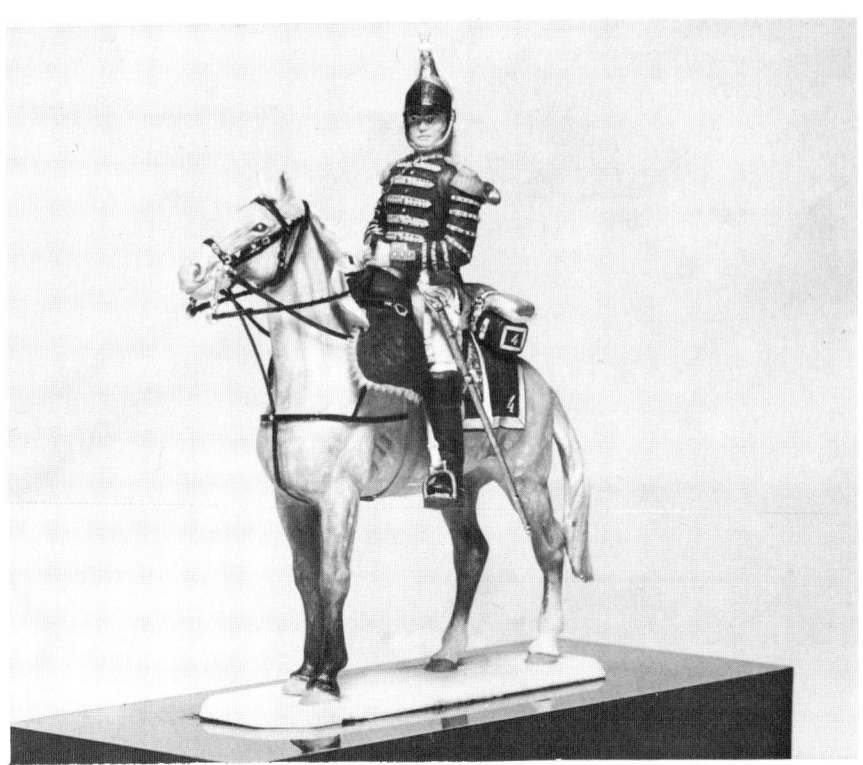

Excellent painting of both dapple horse and the lace detail can be seen on this Dragoon Trumpeter in Imperial Livery which has been constructed straight from a Historex kit.

fixed by Five-Minute Epoxy, smoothly applied over the entire area and well rubbed down. Whether applied from metallic coverings or merely painted with 'silver' paint, the details of rivets and fastenings can be nicely brought out by a gently applied wash of thinned down black. This adheres to ridges, etc, and gives a most realistic effect, akin to the shading and highlighting on a model in ordinary cloth garments. Some of the cheapest of 54 mm figures, the Britain's 'Herald' knights can be transformed in appearance by this simple trick; incidentally these plastic models of knights are moulded in 'silver' polythene and plastic moulded in this colour invariably achieves the effect of body armour better than any amount of 'silver' painting can achieve. So before actually painting any knight figure, assess the quality of its appearance as purchased.

When it comes to painting horses, there are extra problems in that a well-groomed horse has a sheen. One way to do this is to paint the creature with matt colours, and then, when it is entirely dry, paint over the entire creature with matt clear varnish. Despite its title, this varnish is not entirely flat, and gives a very slight sheen which is quite realistic. The semi-matt Railway Enamels, previously mentioned, are also usable if they are well mixed with

Above: Two dark-skinned figures — African female warriors — showing the sheen effect. Left: Larger-than-life view of a 54 mm scale FANY of 1905, showing detail painting. The tight tunic does not involve folds and creases and thus little artificial shading is needed in this case. Models by Arthur Woolford.

matt colours (for instance a semi-matt brown mixed about 2:1 with matt black to give a dark chestnut. This gives a good sheen which is not too glossy. Highlighting, with a touch of white worked in specially round the neck and haunch muscles, is very necessary in darker horses, and shading generally follows the rules for clothing, save that the various muscle and prominent tendons provide the areas which must be shaded. Pictures of horses should be studied to see how shadows form. Horses are a study in themselves, and your research can profitably include perusal of one or other colour guides to horses (there are several books on this theme). Dapple effects can be achieved by painting the creature white or better still off-white, then working in the dapple pattern by 'dry brushing' (working out the brush until only minimal paint remains before applying it to the surface). Tails and manes are matt, and hoofs usually quite glossy.

In all painting, and specially in shading and highlighting, it is better to add colours sparingly; it is easier to add more colour, but always difficult to get rid of too much. It remains to stress that Stage 9 in the painting sequence can be used to good effect to add emphasis to distinctive features. Very fine outlining can pick out buckles and small straps, and garments such as spiral-wound puttees can be greatly enhanced if a fine line is run round them. There is usually a slight shadow round the overlapping turns of puttees, as there is under pocket flaps, so such lining, unless it is over done is not strictly speaking a departure from the real thing.

Figures in the smaller scales, notably 20/25 mm and smaller cannot necessarily be painted with such detail as 30, 40, 54 mm and larger. For a start very fine brushes would be required plus the requisite skill to use them. Most workers in small scales concentrate on the main colours, belts and equipment. Shading is sometimes possible, but face details are difficult to do — lips and dark pin-size blobs for the eyes are usually the best that can be achieved, but much depends on the personal skill of the modeller. Some very tiny model soldiers have been displayed painted with all conceivable detail, and the leading collectors of Flats invariably paint their models with astonishing beauty.

Painting is a skill which comes only with practice, particularly with model soldiers which may present problems even to those used to painting other sorts of scale replicas, like model aircraft. The complete beginner is advised to keep paintwork simple, avoiding any attempts at shading or highlighting on early models if necessary until you get the 'feel' for painting. It is always possible to paint early attempts again later as your skill increases. These techniques can be tried out first on scrap material if desired, but the best way for the beginner to master the art is to plunge in and have a go.

In some types of model, particularly plastic, there is an added aid to painting in those cases where the detail of lace and braid is sharply defined on the figure. Historex models are particularly good for this. Very complicated lace is minutely but neatly moulded in relief and the use of 'dry brushing' with gold paint brings this lace up beautifully with all its delicate tracery, making the job of painting much less formidable than it might at first appear. The 'dry brushing' technique has other uses in figure painting, the major one being the representation of mud and dirt on tunics, boots, and trousers, etc.

Use brass or copper shim or paper

KILTS

fold

Work out pattern first – then cut and fold.

score

shape to figure

COLOURS

Design and paint on paper both sides

Cut out and fold gently with fingers to hang correctly

Cast flags in metal or Plastic

Draw design on paper pattern – fold this to shape and use as guide when painting flag or colour.

DRUMS

Draw and colour on paper – cut out

Trumpet banners, pipe banners and lance pennons from paper

Use same idea as colours above.

Don't forget rims. Make cords and tighteners from paper and cord.

Such work should be judiciously carried out, however; any really heavy application begins to look just what it really is — smears of paint. Avoid 'pure' colours when 'dry brushing' dirt or mud. In other words don't use a colour like dark earth straight from the pot; mix it with a touch of black, white, brown, etc, (according to terrain) to arrive at a fairly neutral colour. Obviously if your diorama terrain was chalky (eg, the Somme, 1916) white would predominate in your 'earth' mix, and in a desert setting ochre might be the main colour used — and for dust and sand the brush application must be very 'dry' indeed.

Colours, guidons, drum banners, and standards offer an interesting challenge. It is easy enough, perhaps, to paint a small lance pennant, but a set of regimental colours carried by a colour party might offer more problems. First, however, bear in mind that from time to time pre-printed sets of colours for 20 mm, 30 mm, and 54 mm are produced by specialist firms, and these are worth snapping up for stock (even if you have no immediate plans for their use), simply because this sort of thing seems to go off the market just when you think you'd like to buy it. One or two commercial firms, notably Britain's, have produced colour party sets over the years with neat card colours included, and these are obviously worth obtaining if you have a penchant for colour guards and parade figures. A few kits have included printed colours in black outline only, for painting by the purchaser, using water colours. Beyond this you will have to make your own. Clearly a good deal of research may be necessary to establish the exact scale size, but several books have appeared over the years, not to mention pre-war cigarette card sets and regimental and corps histories, which have illustrated designs and covered the subject in some detail. Most colours at the carry, and even drum and trumpet banners, develop folds, and this can be useful if fine detail painting is beyond your skill.

The best procedure for making banners or colours of your own is to draw out the design to the exact scale size of good quality fine wove writing paper. It need not be correct in every detail in 54 mm or smaller — clearly tiny 'battle honour' wording cannot be depicted letter for letter unless fine writing is your forte, but the scroll and a representation of the writing can be drawn in. Some modellers then paint the design in model paints (eg, the Humbrol or Airfix types), though others prefer to use water colours applied fairly 'strong'. If model paints are used, great care must be taken in cutting out and folding the flag to hang correctly, as this type of paint flakes off some papers.

Some metal models come with the colour included, made of folded sheet metal or cast in the same metal as the figure. Some plastic figures come with colours moulded in plastic. In this type of model the colour may be moulded at the carry, complete with folds. Sometimes the colour is very much over scale thickness and clumsy or heavy in appearance, in which case the solution is to remove it and replace it with a paper substitute, either the pre-printed or home painted versions as described. Where the moulded colour provided is considered good enough to retain, the problem of painting it arises since the design has to be painted realistically on to a surface with the folds and creases already included. The best answer is to make a paper replica, pencil in the required design, fold it to match the folds and creases in the cast version, and then use the folded paper replica as a guide to the positioning of the design on the hanging flag. This ensures that perspective and the relative positioning of the visible and folded parts of the designs is faithfully reproduced.

The decorative devices commonly painted round bass and tenor drums can be approached in a similar way. Indeed drums can be made easily enough from scratch, cutting slices from wood dowelling of the requisite diameter, or slices from plastic tubing with the 'skins' cut from plastic card. The decorative panelling can be drawn out to scale on paper, the design pencilled in, and the entire panel painted. If you make a mistake, it is easy enough on paper to have a second try. Cut out the design, and glue it round the drum. The cords are then cemented in on top of the paper design using a transparent 'univeral' glue, or Five-Minute Epoxy. Twisted fuse wire (two strands together) can make most realistic cords, but heat-stretched sprue is also effective. On a plastic or metal drum in a kit, the same paper panel technique can be used, but if the cords are moulded integral it will be necessary to file them off, and then fashion new cords after the paper design is in position.

Bagpipe banners, plaids, and kilts offer many problems. They can variously be made from paper, painted as described for flags, cut out and folded as described. Some modellers do the same thing with fine brass shim .005 inches thick (sold in larger hobby stores), and others use toothpaste tubing flattened out. Where one starts with a flat sheet, whatever the material, it is possible to paint out the base colour, then use a mapping pen and coloured inks, or a more elaborate draughtsman's pen, to ink in the design of the plaid very neatly, with ruled lines. It is often necessary to simplify the design, of course, for 54 mm or smaller sizes. Bagpipe banners moulded on a figure are often over scale in thickness and can be replaced with paper to improve the appearance. More usually the kilt and plaid (if any) is moulded satisfactorily on

Colour party of Royal Fusiliers, 1914, constructed by Roy Dilley from Britain's figures. Colours are made from paper as described in text.

Close view of 54 mm German figures show the subtleties of shading, highlighting, and picking out of details, to give effective and realistic results. Models by Roy Dilley.

a figure and the only problem is painting. There is no real short cut other than hand painting, due to the pleated nature of this apparel, but on the other hand the pleating can obscure the fact that the painting of the fine lines of the sett is less than perfect. One tip for beginners is to prefer to model a regiment (eg, the Black Watch) with a dark pattern kilt, since the darker the colours the more potential there is for simplication. In very small scale in 54 mm scale only a slight suggestion of the black sett is needed over the dark green. In fact you can get away quite well by aiming for effect rather than absolute precision and it is worth recalling that the old Britain's models of Highland regiments used to look fairly effective with tartans painted quite crudely by today's standards.

We have said nothing here about painting in oils, gouache, and other modern art materials, save to acknowledge that it can be done. In this book, however, we are concerned with what any average modeller can do, and it must be said at once that while one can confidently buy some tins of model paints and the necessary brushes and get on with painting model figures, use of oil paints and the like requires much more specialised skill and knowledge, and above all practice. If you have had artistic training, the use of these materials may be easy enough. Some excellent work is done by top modellers who walk away with many of the prizes at exhibitions. But many of these modellers are also artists by profession or training. If you want to read more of the hints and tips and methods of those who use oils, gouache, polymer paints and the like, then there is fairly good coverage of this in the Philip Stearns book *How to Make Model Soldiers* (Hamlyn). An important consideration, skills and ability apart, is the cost, for these paints (which you can see in any art supply shop) usually cost considerably more than the ordinary oil-based model paints which have been discussed in this chapter.

'O' Group of staff officers at 8th Army HQ shows that painting can be kept simple yet effective. These John Sandars models are all conversions from cheap plastics. Plain colours of modern combat dress make World War periods a good choice for beginners.

The RN Officer and ratings with Gardner gun are Roy Dilley conversions from Britain's plastic American Civil War figures, with no change in animation or position from the original items. Mini-diorama is fashioned on a small offcut of chipboard.

11: Diorama and Display

JUST as there are many approaches to model soldier collecting, so there are endless ways to show off the completed model. The subject really divides into two—presentation of individual figures and display of an entire collection, or whatever part can be displayed.

Presentation

In its simplest form, the model soldier comes on its own individual base which enables it to stand. The age old method of showing models, lining them up for wargames, or whatever, was simply to consider every piece as an individual item. Traditionally the metal stand was painted green, and modern figures sold individually (in both the 'toy' and 'model' category) carry on in this way. If you plan to display your models individually, you may consider the matter no further. It is pertinent to say, however, that the great range of scenic materials now available makes it possible even to improve on the old-fashioned integral base. When the model is finished in all other respects, just smear the base with cement and sprinkle on scenic flock powder (representing grass or gravel), sand, or fine bird seed, etc, according to choice, and tip off the surplus. Your figure is then standing on a natural looking surface rather than a square or round plastic or metal base. This is particularly effective with 'toy' figures whose plastic origin can be completely disguised if the base is covered like this. The Britain's Detail figures detach from their bases, incidentally and can be cemented to a circular plastic card base if desired before painting takes place. A further variation is to complete the model with no base at all. A very neat circular base can then be made from metal or plastic card which has a covering of Vaupe or Noch grass matt (many other makes are available). The figure is then cemented (after painting) to the 'grass' covered base, and this is very effective due to the superior and realistic texture of the grass with its individual blades. The Vaupe and Noch type grass matts are sold in large hobby shops in a variety of textures, but there are some cheaper alternatives, including green baize or felt, and there are some modern textured coverings which are grass-like, sold in hardware stores.

Some figures in larger scales, such the Series 77 pieces, come with a fairly elaborate cast base which includes a space for a title and some representation of the ground. This type of base can be worked up very satisfactorily with model paints, scenic compounds, or a combination of the two to give a handsome display piece. Plastic plinths have been produced by some makers and it is quite feasible to produce this type of plinth yourself, from scrap wood, sawn, sanded and bevelled as desired, and finished off with varnish or lacquer paint. The larger type of figure looks well on a distinctive plinth. Several modellers have utilised the gift-pack plastic drum in which some brands of cigarette are sold. The drum lid can be used as it comes to form a circular plinth, and some scenic work can be arranged on the top to give a neat and pleasing finish if desired. 54 mm and 77 mm figures are just the right size for

Above: Proof that even the cheapest plastic figures can make realistic additions to a collection; these polythene Airfix 54 mm Germans have been painted straight from the box without alteration of any kind and set in a fine diorama by the makers. Below: A professionally made large scale RHA 13 pdr gun detachment of 1918 made by H. H. Cawood for the Imperial War Museum, London. Note the base, of plywood with simple scenic covering.

Above: Diorama base on chipboard with model rail scenic accessories, for temporary display of models. 20 mm Germans are arranged in an attack scene. Below: Pierre Van Tiechen made this Egyptian temple diorama (built on a board base), with postcards for the wall frieze. Figure is from the Rose range in 54 mm.

this sort of drum. Taking this theme further, some cigarette brands come in a clear plastic cylindrical container, and this forms a fine individual showcase for the model, the entire package being used, upside down, in effect, the lid forming the plinth and the container making the showcase. The use of plastic lids or shallow pots of various types, painted or unpainted as required, means that the average home will provide a source of plinths from what would otherwise be scrap material.

Moving up the scale a little, we come to the very popular small diorama, or 'mini' diorama, which is big enough to enable up to six figures or so to be displayed in some sort of scenic setting. Thus we can have a machine-gun team in action, a sentry being relieved at his box with NCO taking charge, a colour party, a courtyard with seat and two or three figures, a gun and its detachment in action, and endless other 'vignettes' of this type reflecting military life. Some very clever and ambitious work has been done in this field. One or two prize-winners have used small picture frames and built up what amounts to a three-dimensional picture inside in a shallow box with a suitable group. The more usual approach is to take a square or circular piece of wood or chipboard (these can often be purchased as offcuts for a nominal price at hardware stores), and give this a scenic treatment which can range from a covering of grass mat only through to a complicated multi-level effect.

The principals are those familiar to anyone who has seen model rail layouts, though the work involved can be simple. For example just a few stone chips and sand, with perhaps a cactus (in plastic) might make a convincing desert scene. At the other extreme there might be trees, bushes, and a pond. Patching plaster (such as Polyfilla) mixed with a little sawdust or sand makes an excellent 'earth mix' for this type of small diorama. It can be precoloured while mixing to give an earth effect, utilising brown, black, and ochre powder paint—or it can be painted after setting. Scenic work, cork bark for rock, grass matt, and plastic walling, can be purchased at most model rail shops. The German firm of Faller make some fine scenic cards, featuring crazy paving, cobbles, stonework, and the like, embossed in relief and fully coloured. Your scenic finish, for a parade ground scene, might be no more than a covering of Faller cobbles and a suggestion of fencing. One of the pictures in this book shows a regimental group of German cavalry types by Series 77 most effectively displayed on a diorma base which is no more than a plain sheet of paving.

For 54 mm scale Airfix and Timpo make a few 1:32 scale structures specifically for scenic work (eg, a shell-torn 'strongpoint') and these can be nicely worked up and varied. One point to watch with these is that the visible edges of walls may need to be thickened up for added realism—they tend to come with wafer-thin wall. In smaller scales there is a vast range of building kits which may be utilised, mostly in plastic, but also vac-form items by firms like Bellona/Micro-Mold specifically for dioramas, and some realistic 'stone' texture buildings by Ossett Mouldings. There are specific military buildings done in this OO/HO size by Airfix.

After some years of making and collecting, many modellers amass more miniature figures than they can actually display. In addition, models are taken to society exhibitions, and a temporary display base may be needed. This has

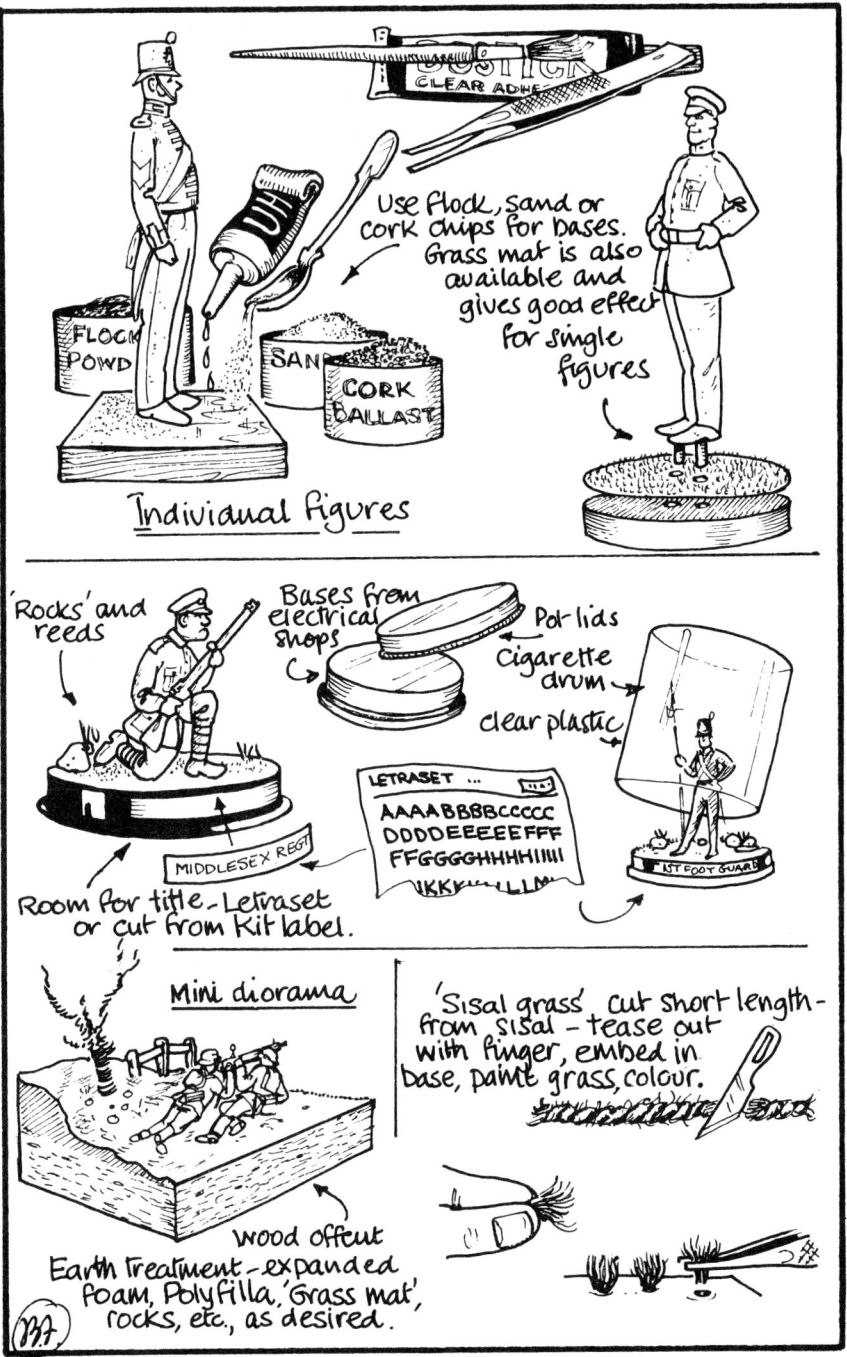

Use Flock, Sand or cork chips for bases. Grass mat is also available and gives good effect for single figures

FLOCK POWD

SAN

CORK BALLAST

BOSTICK CLEAR ADHE

Individual figures

'Rocks' and reeds

Bases from electrical shops

Pot-lids

Cigarette drum

clear plastic

MIDDLESEX REGT

1ST FOOT GUARD

LETRASET ...
AAAABBBBCCCCC
DDDDEEEEEFFF
FFGGGGHHHHIIIII
JJKKK LLLM

Room for title - Letraset or cut from kit label.

Mini diorama

'Sisal grass' cut short length from sisal - tease out with finger, embed in base, paint grass, colour.

wood offcut

Earth treatment - expanded foam, Polyfilla, 'Grass mat', rocks, etc., as desired.

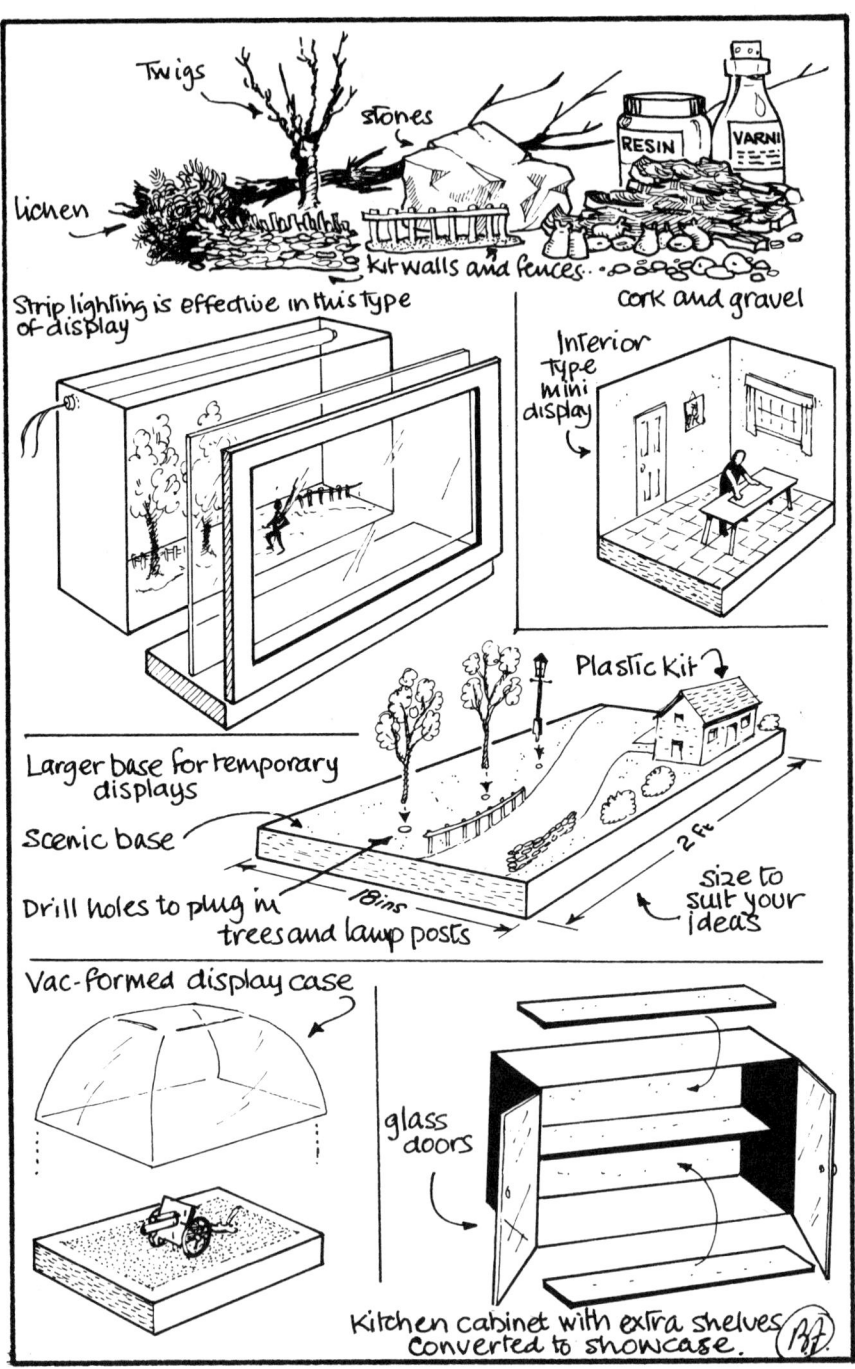

Twigs

stones

RESIN

VARNI

lichen

kit walls and fences

Strip lighting is effective in this type
of display

cork and gravel

Interior
type
mini
display

Plastic kit

Larger base for temporary
displays

Scenic base

Drill holes to plug in
trees and lamp posts

18ins

2 ft

size to
suit your
ideas

Vac-formed display case

glass
doors

Kitchen cabinet with extra shelves
converted to showcase.

led to the development of a slightly larger type of scenic diorama base which does not actually have figures affixed to it permanently. It is generally a fairly neutral sort of scenic terrain; for example, a street, a section of parade ground, a guardroom and barrack gates, a farmyard or village square. Models can then be grouped and displayed on this base for various periods as desired, then removed and replaced by others. Obviously, the base of the individual figure may be visually obtrusive, but this is a small disadvantage in return for the flexibility of the system. Depending on what scenic materials you have to hand, there is the possibility of some variation in the scenic base; some holes can be drilled in concealed parts of the base (eg, behind a bush) so that model trees, lampposts, or other items can be pegged in to vary the appearance from time to time. Many modellers make a selection of different scenic bases so that considerable display variation is possible.

Last of all comes the conventional full-size diorama which may be of considerable size, as much as 6ft long or more, but often rather smaller. This sort of diorama may incorporate very many figures and depict some actual event. In recent years the firm of Hinchliffe have displayed a very fine Rorke's Drift diorama to exhibit their range of Zulu War figures, and featuring well over 100 individual pieces plus a superb replica of the actual buildings and scenery at this epic 1879 action. Museums have long exhibited fine dioramas, and these can give some good ideas for modellers. In 54 mm and larger, big dioramas need a lot of space, of course, and those who favour ambitious diorama work often prefer to work in 20/25 mm or 30 mm where quite extensive work can be done in less than 2ft square. Dioramas are often undertaken as club or group projects. Even in 54 mm scale, some quite compact dioramas can be made if the right subject is chosen. For instance, a whole group of figures, such at those in the Airfix 54 mm scale 'Waterloo Highlanders' box, can be used in a 'form square' type diorama which takes up little more space than the box in which the set is supplied, due to the close proximity of the individual figures in this type of situation.

Display

Once you start to build up your collection, it is pleasing to be able to display your work. If space is a problem you may, of course, be forced to keep all your models in store, but model soldiers do not take up much room individually and most enthusiasts will be able to find some sort of area where the pieces may be safely placed. There are certainly no hard and fast rules for display, except that it is most desirable to keep your complete and painted models free from dust. Dust is a dreadful enemy of the model soldier; not only does it make the piece look shabby, but it leads to the need for frequent dusting which can lead to damage to both detail and paintwork. If you do have (or choose) to leave models exposed to dust, do your dusting very gently with a very soft clean brush.

How you display the models depends on your domestic circumstances. Some modellers have a study, or workroom where showcases or cabinets can be placed at will. Others may have no more than a sideboard or one or two shelves at their disposal. In the latter case, the easiest answer is to find small showcases to cover groups of models. Bell-jars, some fairly cheap vac-formed

Above: Typical accessory set for use in diorama work, in this case from the Tamiya range. Below: An ideal arrangement for displaying models — shallow wall cabinets made by Roy Dilley, seen here with part of his large collection of 54 mm scale figures ('Croydon Advertiser').

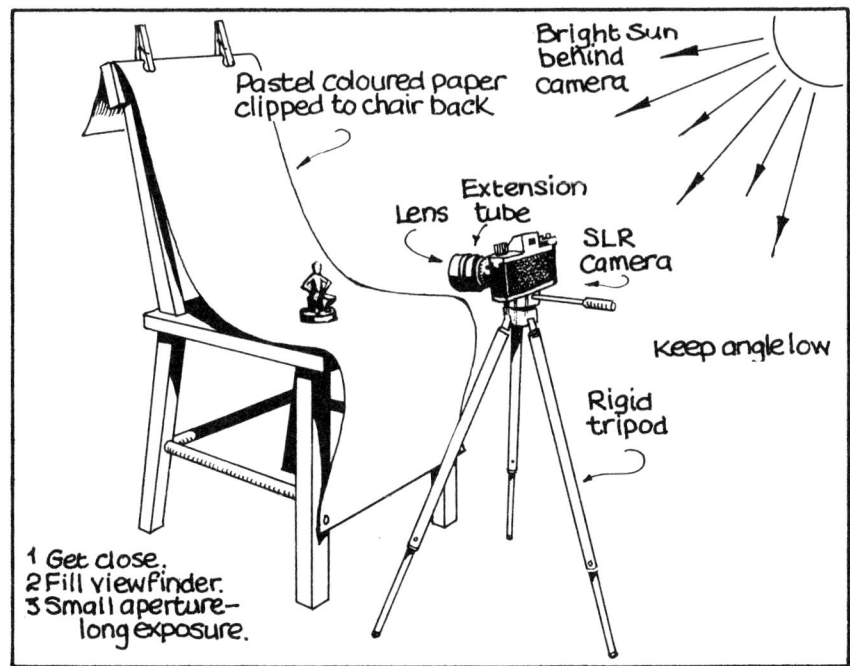

Bright Sun behind camera

Pastel coloured paper clipped to chair back

Extension tube
Lens
SLR Camera

Keep angle low

Rigid tripod

1 Get close.
2 Fill viewfinder.
3 Small aperture–long exposure.

This is the simplest possible set-up for model photography with a SLR camera. A single flood-light close above and in front of the figure would be an alternative for indoors.

covers, orchid boxes (from florists), or transparent plastic food containers are among the items which may be had not too expensively. Space and money permitting, some modellers acquire the old-fashioned type of china cabinet where vast numbers of model soldiers may be arranged to the best advantage. More useful is the wall-hanging cabinet since this takes only a few inches of depth. Given the necessary carpentry skill this type of shallow cabinet, with many shelves, can be constructed at home, complete with hinged or sliding glass doors. Very occasionally this type of cabinet, or the slightly deeper type as used in pharmacy shops and confectioners, may be found on sale. Yet another source of small compact showcase is the kitchen or bathroom cabinet which can be found in unpainted form in some hardware or furnishing stores. These often have hinged or sliding doors in glass and are relatively inexpensive. Extra shelves may be added to increase the storage capacity. One snag here is that most cabinets of this type have frosted or tinted glass doors, and you may need to change these for clear glass. Major Henry Harris, one of the leading model soldier collectors, has made use of several television cabinets of the older wooden type. The complete cabinet is gutted, a shelf arrange inside at a suitable 'viewing' height, and glass is inserted in the original screen space. With a light inside, this makes an attractive setting either for a complete diorama or groups of soldiers. Small strip lighting sets may be purchased quite cheaply in chain stores or electrical shops, specifically for illuminating cabinets or showcases.

If space is limited, you can at least be selective and display only a limited number of models at a time. Storage of models is most easily done by wrapping them in tissues and keeping them in boxes which include some foam packing material.

Model photography

Model photography is a subject in itself, but if you have either a single lens reflex or twin lens reflex camera, plus a tripod and a suitable close-up device (extension tubes for a SLR, 2 or 3 dioptre auxiliary lens set for a TLR), consider making photographs of your models. It is interesting to keep a photographic record of your work in itself, but if you make and show colour slides you'll find that model soldiers can make spectacular slides subjects. An easy standard set-up for photographing one or two figures at a time is shown in the diagram. You can take good colour outside on a sunny day, though if you own floodlights, you can of course work indoors. Exposure times depend on the film, lighting, and other factors. However, with an ASA 64 colour slide film, f/8 at 1/60 second, using a 20 mm extension tube, would be a typical exposure for a single figure photographed against a plain background outdoors in bright sunshine. Consult the leaflet given with the film and the extension tubes, and use metering if available. Bear in mind that depth of field is critical in close-up work so go for smaller apertures (f/8 or smaller) and slower speeds, rather than wide apertures and faster speeds.

AWAITING THE FINAL CHARGE

A fine 'mini' diorama by Norman Abbey is a classic of its type. Two discs of plywood form the base in this case. The titling is from dryprint transfer. The base can be stained, varnished, painted, or polished as required, and felt or Fablon-type covering underneath can be added if desired to prevent scratching of furniture.

APPENDIX

1: Specialist suppliers

Many of the models and accessories mentioned in this book are widely available through model stockists and toy shops. Included in this category are the products of Airfix, Aurora, Timpo, Humbrol, Testor, Joy, Britain's, Tamiya, and Riko. All the types of adhesive and fillers listed are sold either in model shops or in hardware or 'do it yourself' stores, and you may find alternative brands to those mentioned — the dealer will advise if in doubt. Most hobby shops which concentrate on model rail equipment stock a good range of scenic materials, intended for model railways but equally applicable to military dioramas; flock powder (or scatter material) is available under many brand names, as is lichen, cork bark, and assorted types of grass mat and embossed or printed 'stone' paper. For 54 mm scale, look for farmyard accessories produced by Britain's and Timpo, sold in most toy shops. Numerous plastic building kits are available in the small scales, and some special military ones are available from Airfix in 1:32 scale.

In addition to the above, some, but by no means all, model shops specialise in model figures of the 'collector' type and most of these advertise in *Military Modelling* magazine. If you have no stockist of this type in your area, mail order from a stockist is advised. Some makers of model figures sell direct by post. Any listing here would soon date, but some important addresses of suppliers mentioned in this book are given below:

Historex Agents, 3 Castle Street, Dover, Kent, England (Historex kits, and extensive variety of Historex components sold separately; also paints and prints, etc; list and catalogues available direct).

Rose Models, 45 Sundowne Road, Charlton, London, SE7 (metal 'collector' figures and kits in 20 mm, 30 mm, 54 mm, and cast metal spare heads, arms, etc).

Greenwood & Ball Ltd, 61 Westbury Street, Thornaby on Tees, Tees-side, England (this firm markets Greenwood & Ball, Lasset, Minot and some other types, and also offers many spare parts for 54 mm scale, useful for conversion work — lists available direct).

Model Figures & Hobbies, Lower Balloo Road, Groomsport, Co Down, Northern Ireland (importer of French Segom plastic figure kits and components — lists available direct).

Hinchliffe Models Ltd, Meltham, Huddersfield, England (major maker of cast figures in 20 mm, 25 mm, 54 mm, 75 mm, plus many accessories — catalogue available direct).

2: Some societies

Recent years have seen a big proliferation in the number of clubs and societies which have been formed for military enthusiasts. Many concentrate on wargaming or the study (and sometimes the re-enactment) of majoɪ periods of military history. Virtually every issue of *Military Modelling* brings news of newly-formed clubs of various sorts. It is not practicable to repeat all these here and such information dates rapidly due to changes of officials and their addresses. However, here are some nationally known societies of general interest to all.

British Model Soldier Society; J. Ruddle (Hon Sec), 22 Priory Gardens, Hampton, Middx. BMSS now has many area and affiliated groups, and produces a useful journal for members. Details and area secretaries from the Hon Sec.

Military Historical Society; J.W.F. Gaylor (Hon Sec), 7 East Woodside, Leighlands, Bexley, Kent, England. Not strictly a modelling society, this is, however, the foremost club for the student of military history, producing a much respected journal.

Miniature Figure Collectors of America; Blair C. Stonier (Hon Sec), 2555 Haverford Road, Ardmore, Pa 19003, USA. The United States equivalent of BMSS.

Military Historical Society (of USA); Hon Sec, Box 639, Times Square Station, New York 36, NY, USA. The United States equivalent of MHS.

Send a stamped addressed envelope when writing for information from these addresses.

3: Journals and books

Many of the clubs and societies produce their own journals for members. There are a number of well-known magazines widely available, and of these the following usually contain articles of interest to model soldier enthusiasts:

Military Modelling (MAP Ltd).
Battle (MAP Ltd).
Airfix Magazine (PSL Publications).
Soldier (HMSO).
Armies & Weapons (Interconair).
Scale Modeler (Challenge Publications, USA).
Soldier (Challenge Publications, USA).
Military Modeler (Challenge Publications, USA).

Very many books have been published, both on model soldier making and collecting, and on uniform information in general. Some important books are mentioned in the text. In addition, the following is a select list of books, or series of books, of good reference value for model soldier enthusiasts.

Almarks series (many were published in the 1970-74 period, but some are out of print; recent titles cover famous battles).

Osprey 'Men at Arms' (many published since 1971, covering individual regiments of units, all with colour plates and illustrations).

Blandford Press 'Encyclopaedia in Colour' series (many titles covering periods of history or arms of service, eg, *Uniforms of the American Revolution, Infantry Uniforms 1742-1855,* and widely available).

Seeley Service series of books by Major R.M. Money Barnes *(Regiments* and Uniforms of the British Army, Scottish Regiments, Military Uniforms of Britain and The Empire, The British Army of 1914 and others). Castermann series of books by L. & F. Funcken (covering the Napoleonic period, 1914-18 war, and soldiers of all periods — these are heavily illustrated in colour and written in French, but the latter volumes are published in an English language edition as mentioned in Chapter 6).

Below: Simple but effective display base by John Sandars. Photo was taken using exactly the set up shown on page 107.

Superb diorama work by Historex artists R. Gillet and E. Lievefvre is typical of what can be done in a traditional glass fronted showcase. Background is hand painted.